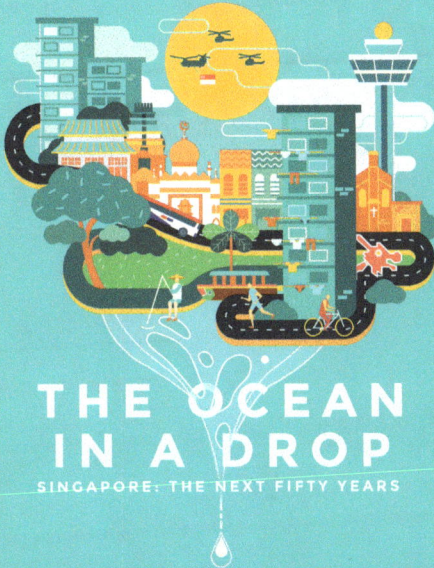

THE OCEAN IN A DROP
SINGAPORE: THE NEXT FIFTY YEARS

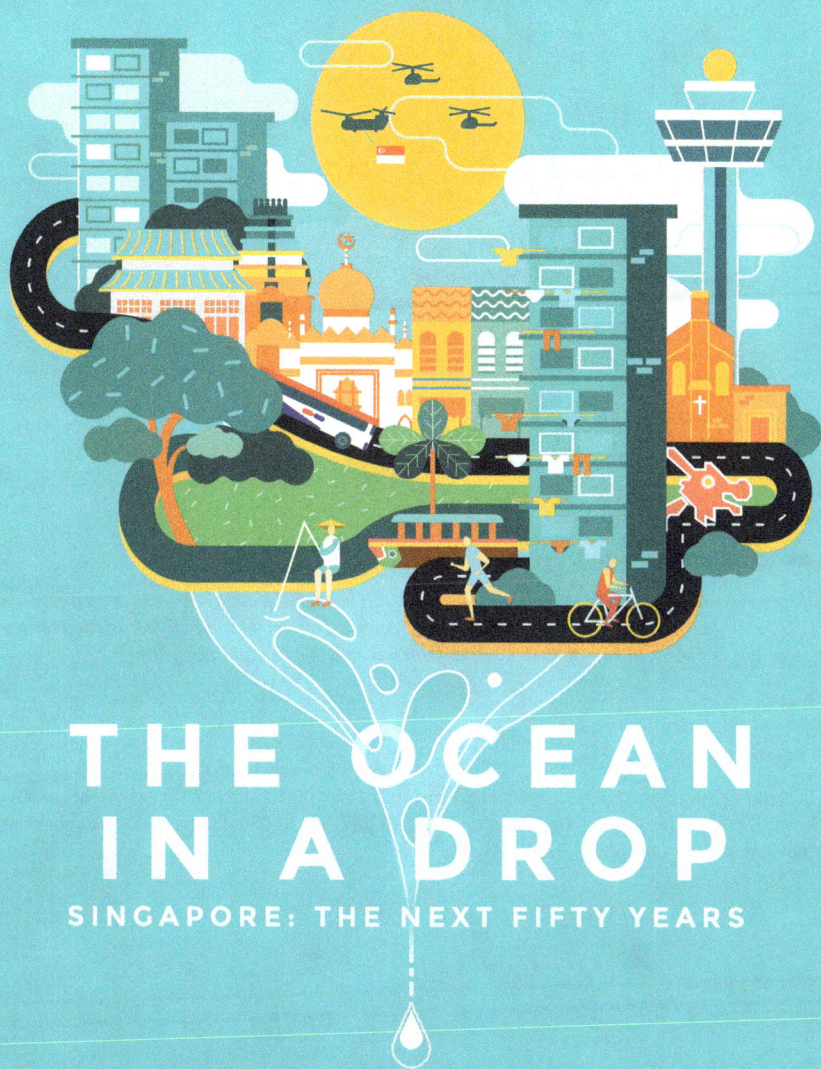

THE OCEAN IN A DROP

SINGAPORE: THE NEXT FIFTY YEARS

HO KWON PING

Published by

World Scientific Publishing Co. Pte. Ltd.

5 Toh Tuck Link, Singapore 596224

US office: 27 Warren Street, Suite 401-402, Hackensack, NJ 07601

UK office: 57 Shelton Street, Covent Garden, London WC2H 9HE

British Library Cataloguing-in-Publication Data
A catalogue record for this book is available from the British Library.

THE OCEAN IN A DROP
Singapore: The Next Fifty Years

ISBN 978-981-4730-17-4
ISBN 978-981-4730-18-1 (pbk)

In-house Editor: Sandhya Venkatesh

Typeset by Stallion Press
Email: enquiries@stallionpress.com

You are not a drop in the ocean.

You are the entire ocean, in a drop.

— *Rumi* (Persian poet, 1207–1273)

Dedicated to my family:

My Parents,

My Wife

My Children

And my Grandchildren

CONTENTS

FOREWORD

When I agreed to be the first S R Nathan Fellow for the Study of Singapore I had not the faintest idea what I was up for. Mr Janadas Devan, Director of IPS, called me and said that "you only need to talk about anything related to Singapore". Then he said that Mr S R Nathan had wanted me to be the inaugural candidate for his namesake fellowship. Since I have the highest respect for Mr Nathan, I readily agreed.

But I had no idea of what to speak on — and sound reasonably intelligent at the end of it all — for what eventually became a total of more than ten hours stretching across five lectures over nine months. Unlike an academic, public servant, professional, or diplomat who has made a career from some specialised intellectual pursuits, I had no such credentials or competencies.

Or indeed, even a linearly-progressing career development path to draw upon: my education had not prepared me for any kind of domain expertise. I had attended three universities but took nine years to even attain a simple Bachelor's degree in economics. I had been a journalist and wrote on an eclectic range of topics but without being an authority on any particular subject. I had founded a hotel company without the slightest knowledge of the hospitality industry except having been an avid backpacker in my youth. And most improbably, I had been tasked to start a management university after having been kicked out of Stanford University as an undergraduate student.

But one of my incorrigible attributes, which has brought me as much trouble as tribulation, is a certain sceptical curiosity about a lot of things. I have told many audiences — mostly young people — that the dominant driving force in my intellectual life is the most subversive and yet most liberating three-letter word in the English language: WHY.

Asking WHY has led me to be thrown out of Stanford, jailed in California, barred from entry to the USA for two decades, and detained in Singapore under the Internal Security Act (ISA). I have certainly gotten into trouble, starting from childhood and into adult life, because asking WHY of things has often gotten me labelled as a rebel or troublemaker.

But my intention has never been to challenge something for its own sake. Indeed, asking WHY and then following the question to where it leads you to, often actually takes you full circle, back to where you started. But if that happens then all the more will your original belief, now reinforced by independent and critical enquiry, be stronger and rooted in self-searching. Asking WHY has led me to reinforce several fundamental convictions and discover some innovative insights.

So that was the attitude I took towards the IPS-S R Nathan Lectures series. I wanted to ask WHY certain things are as they are in Singapore, or WHY NOT, and follow my own instincts to some possible answers. And it has been a satisfying personal journey.

Unlike someone writing a book with a well-conceived theme and set of arguments, I was winging it the entire way. With a roughly one-month gap between lectures, I started thinking about the next lecture a week after the last one was delivered. I was only required early on to decide the broad themes for each lecture. Flummoxed and somewhat desperate, I simply adopted the not very original idea of simply copying the IPS' own research clusters. And that was how I arrived at the very impressive-sounding themes of: Politics and Governance; Economy and Business; Security and Sustainability; Demography and Family; and finally Society and Identity.

Having chosen the themes, my approach was to ask questions along a 50-year time frame, so that I would not be distracted by any particular issues of the day, in order to ask more fundamental, first-principle questions. I looked for the figurative elephants in the room – silent, inescapably huge and looming presences which most people pretend don't exist simply because they're ignored. I saw my task as identifying and describing the elephants, and encouraging people to think about them.

For the **first** lecture, on politics and governance, it was clear that the unspoken subject in the back of most people's minds concerned the longevity of the PAP. History has not been kind to parties which founded a nation in a democracy — most do not last longer than the half century which the PAP has already celebrated. The PAP is hardly following the pattern — it remains vigorous, generally popular, in full control of the nation and people's minds as Singapore celebrates its half century of independence and mourns the death of its first, founding prime minister.

But under what conditions might Singapore change and the PAP find itself unpopular and lose power? Competence and incorruptibility, rather than popularity, have been the hallmark of the PAP. Can the second, third, fourth generation of leaders and electorate, completely different from the founding and second generation, find a common vision, purpose and social compact to take Singapore to the next half century? And if not, is the opposition ready to take up the mantle?

The **second** lecture, on economy and business, was less dramatic. I essentially analysed the fundamental economic strategy of Singapore and concluded that it remained sound and relevant even as our own economy and that of the world, changed rapidly, so long as we continue to broaden and deepen our capabilities in the various industry clusters which we adopted decades ago. I also proposed a fundamental rethink of the role of the Housing & Development Board (HDB) in the next 50 years — to be more of a housing price regulator than the monopoly developer of public housing.

The **third** lecture on security and sustainability made the suggestion that we should start a form of national service for women. As with the HDB issue, I was hardly proposing any immediate measures. But I did feel that some form of national service focussing more on civil defence and community care, rather than on military preparedness, would benefit both our women and our rapidly aging society, as well as create a national mind-set which might accept military service for women, should the need ever arise in the future. In subsequent talks to student gatherings, I also made this proposal and was encouraged by the response, especially from young women (so long as the NS for them did not disrupt their studies).

Because I defined security through the three dimensions of external, internal and civil security, I also recommended changes to the ISA and a suspension of caning. The media seemed more interested that as an ex-political detainee I did not recommend the abolition of the ISA. I would have preferred a deeper discussion on caning as possibly a punishment we can start to phase out over the next 50 years.

By the time I got to the **fourth** lecture I was becoming a bit of a policy wonk. The concept of "retirement adequacy" — whether Singaporeans would have enough savings to tide them through a secure and relatively comfortable retirement — was a hot topic. It dealt with a plethora of government measures, including but not limited to the Central Provident Fund or CPF. After reviewing the various measures I felt that we needed to return to an over-arching concept which would be simple enough for the general public to understand, because the many measures which had been introduced in the last five decades were complex and sometimes over-lapping but also "under-lapping" in several areas. So I proposed a "CPF-Plus" concept. And to promote procreation I essentially looked at the success of some Nordic countries and asked whether we should dare to try the same measures here.

My last lecture was soon after the death of Mr Lee Kuan Yew[1]. Against the poignant backdrop of national mourning and the new-found sense of national unity, I returned to a theme I had mentioned in my first lecture: that we search for a cohesive diversity rather than a singular and perhaps even simplistic national identity.

Throughout the lectures I have assiduously stuck to the issues and kept myself out of the picture. But I ended the lecture series with a short sharing of my personal journey towards identity, with the hope that sharing

---

[1] Also referred to by his initials LKY in this book.

our individual stories and celebrating our similarities and differences is the starting point of cohesive diversity.

Singapore's singular success in the past 50 years has been marked by pragmatic and appropriate policies enacted without the hindrances of participatory democracy. In the next 50 years, the mixture of politics and policy may require inevitable trade-offs such as lower efficiency in public administration in return for higher public participation. Our society will only continue to prosper if more public intellectuals, members of civil society, and the general public will enter the marketplace of ideas and subject themselves and their ideas to public scrutiny and even possible ridicule, for the goal of a better society.

My contribution to the construction of this marketplace is the IPS-Nathan Lectures series, which for me started as a journey towards academic respectability and ended up as a collection of (hopefully) provocative speculations about and suggestions for the future prosperity of Singapore.

It is my fervent hope that as we progress towards a more enlightened but also socially responsible civil society, the S R Nathan Fellowship and its public IPS-Nathan Lectures series, will become an important fixture in everyone's calendar. Future S R Nathan Fellows can play an important role not only in creating the bridge between civil society, academia, and government, but also in setting the agenda for dialogue — and even possibly rancorous debate.

To quote from this book:

> *In the next 50 years — the Singapore after Mr Lee Kuan Yew — the line between leader and follower will start to blur; we will not just be disciplined and unquestioning followers. Our leaders will walk amongst and not ahead of us; they will be part of, and not simply lead, the national conversation. Other people may march to their own drumbeat and at their own pace. We may look from the outside, to be less orderly and consensual than in the past. But I certainly hope that what will never change from one generation to another, is the passion to make this country continue to succeed, to be proud of who we have been, are, and will be, and to revel in the cohesive diversity that makes us all Singaporeans — whatever that word means to each of us. ... After all, civil society is not a disciplined army; it is not an organised orchestra producing the soothing melodies of a lovely symphony. It is a loud cacophony of voices, of disorganised aspirations, of an exciting market place of ideas.*

I have in particular been encouraged by how my lectures seem to have resonated with many young people. As Janadas observed after the final lecture, audiences usually dwindle towards the end of a series and only retirees with time on their hands still attend, but for this series, audience size increased over time, and the proportion of young people also increased.

This is undoubtedly helped by the series of informal discussions at my home, my daughter's home and other casual places, with my children's friends and others from different segments of civil society. My very capable and idealistic research assistant Andrew Yeo — whose own personal history is an encouraging story of how potentially marginalised young people can, through sheer determination and ability, build their dreams — was instrumental in organising some of these sessions and in helping in my research.

I have already acknowledged at the end of my last lecture, the people who made this lecture series possible for me — Janadas and the selection committee, Mr S R Nathan and my family.

It remains for me to dedicate this book. I am indebted to my parents — my father Ho Rih Hwa and my mother Li Lien Fung — for it was the stories of their own youthful idealism and activism which sowed the seeds of my own forays into asking WHY and sometimes getting into trouble.

Of course, the sometimes unhappy consequences of some of my more headstrong actions are all due to my own inclinations and they bear no responsibility. Indeed, I could only understand when I became a parent, and now a grandfather, how hard and painful it is to not intervene excessively in the lives of your children and tell them what to do. It was the wisdom of my parents to always accept and love me even when I was wayward and headstrong, that gave me the time and space to find my own answers to the eternal question of WHY.

To my lifelong partner and best friend — Claire — my deep gratitude for 38 years of backpacking and sharing ideas and ideals, which resulted in her memorable one-liner about me: "a socialist in his heart and a capitalist in his pocket". To my three children and their spouses, my thanks for introducing me to the concerns of their generation, as well as the many hours spent discussing issues which appear in this book. And finally I dedicate this book to my grandchildren — the first of whom was born a few months ago — who shall be the true inheritors of the next 50 years.

As for the title of this book? The conclusion of my last lecture perhaps explains it:

> The 13th century Persian poet Rumi once wrote something which should speak to each of us. He wrote, "You are not a drop in the ocean. You are the entire ocean, in a drop."
>
> In other words, you are not a cog in the system, a grain of sand, or a drop in the ocean. In each of you is the whole of Singapore. Each of you represents the collective identities and histories which make up our ocean and on which we shall continue our journey together.

We are each of us, and indeed Singapore itself also, the entire ocean in a drop.

Ho Kwon Ping
Singapore, August 24, 2015.

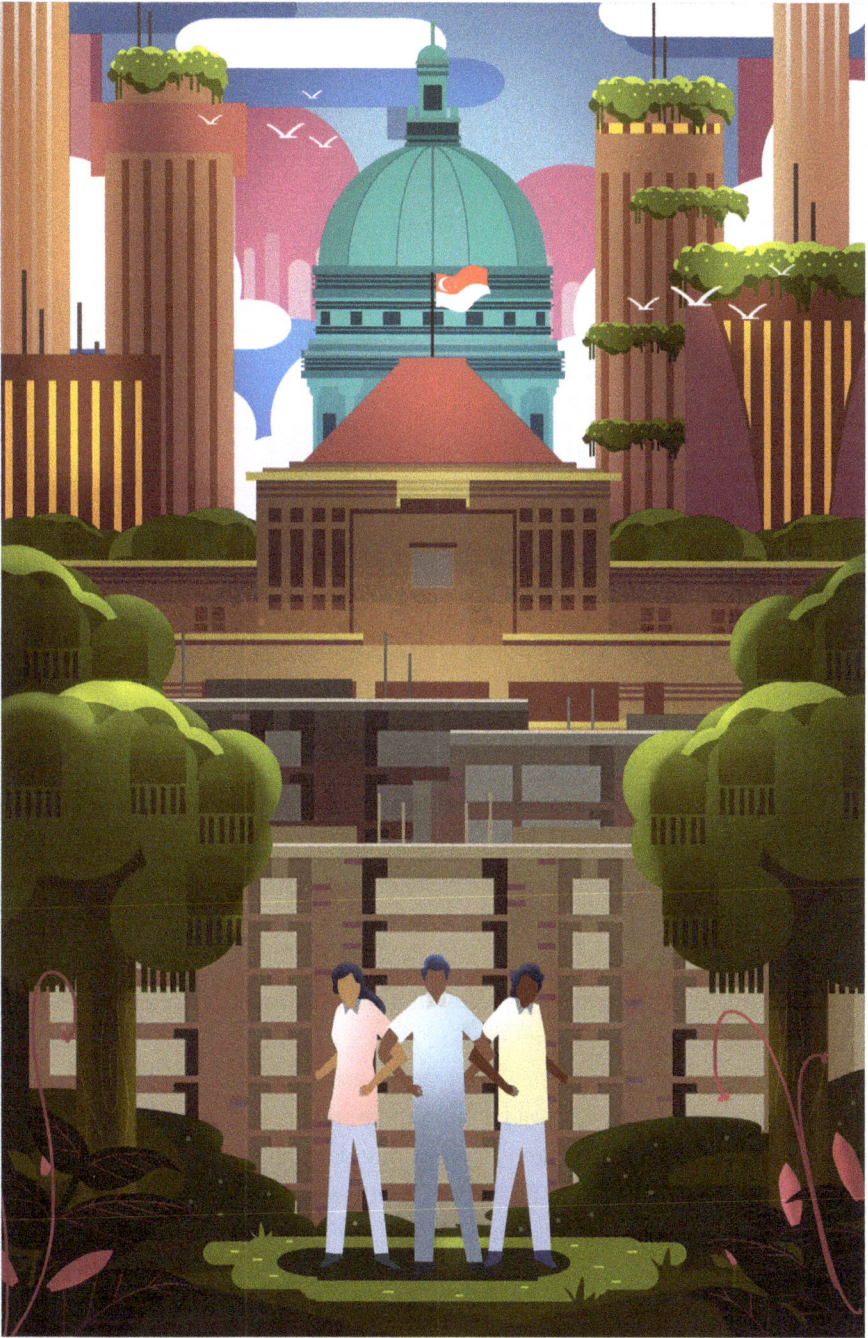

LECTURE I

POLITICS AND GOVERNANCE

G ood evening and welcome to the first of five lectures in the IPS-Nathan Lectures series.

I am very honoured and humbled to be the first S R Nathan Fellow for the Study of Singapore, and I think Mr Nathan truly represents the very best values of the pioneer generation of which he ranks among its most illustrious representatives, and I'd like you to join me to acknowledge his presence here this evening.

When asked to undertake this fellowship my first reaction was a bemused surprise. I've been called a lot of very bad names in my lifetime but never an academic. So I thought I might as well try that word on for size. And contrary to what Ambassador Tommy Koh said, I didn't quite see this as an award; having to prepare for these lectures has taken away my best pastime — which is watching movies on long plane rides. So I'll be very happy when this fellowship is over so that I can go back to watching movies on flights. I am not an academic, as anybody would know; it took me nine years and three universities in three different countries, to just secure a simple Bachelor's degree.

But on the other hand, I am not totally unqualified either. I first embarked on the study of Singapore in 1974 — some 40 years ago — as a bright-eyed, idealistic but somewhat naive 22-year old journalist. Although that particular career ended somewhat unpropitiously, the journey of discovery has continued and I have approached my citizenship as both a right and a responsibility.

Many of you people in the audience, the younger people, are not much older than I was at that time, and although the world and Singapore with it, has changed a lot, I hope you too will engage with the life of this nation and society with an existential passion rather than a cynical apathy.

Every Singaporean knows the significance of this year — the 50th anniversary of our independence. We do have indeed much to be proud of; the Singapore Story is all about the creation and then sustainable continuation, of what can only be described as an improbable nation.

How we did it, however, is not the focus of my lectures, though of course understanding history is vital to foresee the future. I don't want to look backwards, but rather, forward to the next fifty years. I will refer to past events only as background to illustrate the foreground, and will simply assume that everyone here has a pretty broad knowledge of Singapore's history.

> **The Singapore Story is all about the creation and then sustainable continuation, of what can only be described as an improbable nation.**

In addition, I will use data very sparingly, partly because I am not good at research, but mainly because I prefer to be provocative and speculative, and as a wise editor I used to have once told me, never let facts get in the way of a good story!

My main motivation for being an S R Nathan Fellow is to stimulate discussion amongst the younger Singaporeans below 35 years. I hope that this will be an interactive dialogue, where we can collectively explore some of the issues I will be raising.

The five broad topics I propose to cover are: for the first lecture, Politics and Governance; the second will be on Economy and Business. The three remaining topics will be Society and Identity; Demography and Family, and Security and Sustainability. In what sequence these will be addressed, I haven't yet figured out, and I don't know how many of you will actually follow me through to the last lecture.

But, shall we start?

The Three Elephants

To set the stage, I would like to make three major observations which will fundamentally orientate the direction and content of this entire series of lectures. I call them my three elephants in the room, which no one can fail to notice even if they make not a squeak of noise.

The first but not always recognised elephant is the fact that national sovereignty can never be assumed and the external environment can certainly turn hostile in the next 50 years. That we have had a consecutive streak of 50 years of uninterrupted economic growth and national sovereignty is not an immediate guarantee that our grandchildren will have the same good fortune.

Ironically, it is in prolonged periods of peace that a national identity needs to be forged even more vigorously. History has shown that nations can decline and fall entirely due to internal decay. Without an external threat to galvanise people, the unravelling of social cohesion becomes easier. This is one theme that will run through my lectures; namely, internal cohesion will be even more important, and perhaps more difficult to achieve, than in the first half century, when external challenges united us all.

For now, I will simply assume that Singapore will still exist in 50 years' time. But we should not take this assumption for granted and in a later talk on security and sustainability, I will examine the challenges to this assumption.

The second elephant is the obvious question: after stunning economic success, what next? Another 50 years of 3–5% economic growth? What is the second act of this great Singapore miracle?

Some observers have argued that Singapore's best days have passed, because it has reached economic prosperity and there is very little to motivate the present versus the pioneer generation. Middle age flab is, therefore, the cost of maturity, so this argument goes. Others argue that economic growth by itself is a sufficient vision or motivator of people: being doubly or triply richer than now is the prize for hard work.

My answer — assumption really — is that neither is the case. Instead, I think we are at a watershed moment in history whereby our economic prosperity now allows the younger generation the opportunity to realise their society's full potential beyond just the economic realm. As spectacular growth rates taper, the vision for a new Singapore can now embrace a more holistic spectrum.

Because the foundations of economic growth and the pillars of political stability have already been laid, today's young generation can — and will — define and then set out to achieve its own definition of what a developed society means in terms of social justice, an egalitarian culture, political maturity, cultural creativity, and all the other markers of the truly exceptional nation which we can be.

And so, far from having peaked, the best is yet to be.

If we do not accept, almost as a point of faith, that our economic progress must now be matched by a more holistic maturation in other spheres of life, and that this flowering of the Singapore garden is the central task of the younger generation, then we are fated to either decline through thoughtless hubris, or flounder in equally thoughtless self-doubt and anxiety.

> **Our economic progress must now be matched by a more holistic maturation in other spheres of life, and this flowering of the Singapore garden is the central task of the younger generation**

It becomes obvious, then, that it is in the domestic socio-cultural and political realms that change will be the most evident and the most dramatic in the next 50 years. These changes will also involve a process of continual self-invention, so that the Singapore narrative, while hopefully remaining vibrant and relevant in a constantly evolving world, may not necessarily resemble what it was before.

It will not be a tension-free evolution and we will see more heated, so-called culture wars where the government will hopefully not intervene in a heavy-handed and patriarchal manner, but instead allow players from a wide spectrum of civil society to engage and find some mutually acceptable resolution between themselves. This journey towards socio-political and cultural maturity will, in my view, define the next two decades.

For example, the quote attributed to the French philosopher Voltaire as the hallmark of a free society, and I quote *"I disapprove of what you say, but I will defend to the death your right to say it"* is an attitude which should be held fervently by all sides of the political spectrum, including those — from angry bloggers to defensive ministers — who tend to deprecate people rather than respectfully disagree with their views.

Now, the third elephant in the room is equally big and obvious: the biggest player in our political drama before and after independence.

It is widely acknowledged that the People's Action Party (PAP)'s dominance of not only the political process, but almost the entire national culture, was in large part the reason for Singapore's rise from Third to First World in a single generation. The flip side, however, is that this very same dominance is also a main reason for concern in the next 50 years. Can that dominance be maintained? If so, how? And if not, what are the possible changes and ramifications?

Whither the PAP: Some Scenarios

As I will discuss the two other elephants in later lectures, let's now look more closely at the last elephant. Incidentally, I should note that I'm happy to choose a more regal animal like a lion or dragon, or more cuddly like a panda bear, but note, please, all of you, that I consciously did not choose a dinosaur, because it would not be taken very well.

Like other political parties which also founded the nation, the PAP started as a political movement, then a governing party, and finally a national institution with an impact on every sphere of life.

Whereas similar parties in non-democratic nations have no problems extending their longevity by simple fiat — as in North Korea, Cuba, Zimbabwe — the PAP has to legitimise its primacy through periodic general elections. The fact that it has won so many elections so overwhelmingly has made some people perhaps too blasé or cynical about election outcomes.

However, the drama of the last elections for Parliament and President is certainly proof that outcomes are by no means guaranteed.

If the saying that a fortnight is an eternity in politics is true, then 50 years is almost unimaginably long and, therefore, unpredictable. There will be at least three to four new prime ministers who have not even entered politics today. In only 20 more years, the youngest minister today will be retiring and there will remain no more politicians who have any working memory of today's leaders, much less the founding generation.

In the history of young nations, this is the most precarious period of transition, when new generations who do not have the slightest personal memories of or connections to the founding generation, take on the mantle of leadership.

I grew up only knowing slightly the first generation leaders, who were my parents' age and some of whom they knew well as friends. But their passion, dedication and sacrifices were real to us, even though they were already becoming the stuff of legends. To my children, all these people — their ideals, values, and exemplary lives — are all just historical footnotes in school textbooks. Passing on policies is easy; transferring ideals and values requires continual collective connections between generations of living, breathing people.

The history of Third World economies striving towards First World economic and socio-political maturity is replete with failures, running the entire A to Z spectrum, from Argentina to Zimbabwe.

To achieve consistent economic growth with broad-based gains for its entire people has already been a rarely scaled hurdle. To maintain exemplary, transparent governance with an entrenched ethos of incorruptibility is even harder. The PAP has enabled Singapore to rise to the top of the list of successful newly-independent states with these two accomplishments.

Its third challenge is not to just remain in power, nor to maintain its one-party dominance and deny the opposition its self-described role as a "co-driver" of the nation, but to do so in a manner which ensures that the party truly renews itself and retains its original vitality, vibrancy and vigor.

If history is anything to go by, this last task will be very daunting. History has not been very encouraging to political parties after three or four generations. Sustained periods of power breeds complacency and hubris, which are always the seeds of self-destruction.

The PAP has been in power for 56 continuous years, starting from its victory in the 1959 Legislative Assembly elections. The longest continuously ruling party in a democratic nation is Mexico, where the Institutional Revolutionary Party (PRI) lasted for 71 continuous years before it lost control of government.

What about the experience of other parties which founded nation-states? The Colorado party of Paraguay lasted 61 years before it was ousted. The Israeli Labor party ruled over 26 years of coalition governments before it also lost power. Nearer home in Asia, the record is even shorter. The Kuomintang of Taiwan or the Republic of China, lasted 56 years before it was voted out. The Congress Party of India, which led its independence movement, lasted 49 continuous years. The Liberal Democratic Party of post-war Japan, governed for 38 years before it fell.

The fact is, democratically elected ruling parties have generally floundered after about half a century to three-quarters of a century. They become corrupt, riven by internal strife, and eventually prompt a previously loyal electorate to vote them out.

Ironically, however, an electoral loss often enables drastic internal reforms to occur and new reformers to gain control of the party. This new leadership, coupled with disillusionment with the opposition turned governing party, brings the founding party back to power, and a dynamic equilibrium comprising a multi-party pendulum becomes the norm. The present ruling parties in Taiwan, Japan, Korea and Mexico, are all versions of this same story.

So this has been the historical trend, but it is not to say that political precedents are as immutable as the laws of physics. In another 15 years — 2030 — which is about three more elections away, the PAP will overtake the record of Mexico's PRI as the longest continuously ruling party. That, I think, is very likely to happen, as it has not exhibited the signs of moral exhaustion and the onset of decay which these other parties already reached by their middle age. Prime Minister Lee Hsien Loong is still robust in his 60s, has an acute sense of the future of Singapore and remains overwhelmingly popular. The PAP has openly signalled an intention to develop organisational renewal and bring in different types of leaders than in the past. And the most insidious feature of political longevity — corruption — has shown no signs of surfacing yet.

But can this longevity stretch beyond 70 years to 80, 90, 100? If the PAP can buck the trends of history, it will have set a new paradigm of longevity. And it has already set new paradigms of governance in other areas, so it is not an impossible goal, but possibly more difficult than earlier achievements.

Electoral politics going forward will be increasingly uncertain and difficult to predict. Unlike the dynamic equilibrium of a two-party-dominant system, where the political pendulum regularly swings from one ruling party to another, Singapore's equilibrium is stable, but static. There is no precedent by which a ruling party has renewed itself through defeat in the polls, simply because the PAP has never lost.

In other democracies, an entire nation self-corrects through one party taking over from another quite regularly. Obama after Bush, Blair after Thatcher, Cameron after Blair, these are all the pendulum swings of a dynamically stable equilibrium. Singapore after the PAP — the idea is almost unthinkable. And yet, for the good of the nation, think it we must.

One thought that I've put forward is that there are only three basic scenarios for the PAP in the next 50 years:

1. **The Status Quo Scenario**. As it suggests, this scenario sees the PAP controlling say 85% to 90% of Parliamentary seats, with the opposition controlling at most a dozen seats or so. This is regardless of the popular vote, where support for the PAP has dropped to a record low of 60% and may even decline further, because although the popular vote for the PAP has been declining, it is really control of Parliament that matters.

2. **The Dominant Party Scenario**. The PAP retains control of an important two-thirds majority, or at the very least, an absolute majority, of Parliamentary seats. This is closer to the situation in Malaysia. Assuming there are still around only 90 to 100 seats in Parliament, that means in a dominant party scenario, the opposition parties will control around 30 to 50 seats, which is almost unimaginable today.

3.   **Two-Party Pendulum Scenario.** A single opposition party or a coalition wins an election. Power then shifts between the PAP and the second major party in Singapore. This is pretty much the norm in all other developed, liberal democracies. A variant of this scenario is that the PAP splits and new coalitions form which alternate in winning elections.

These scenarios are quite obvious and commonsensical. It is the likelihood of the various scenarios occurring which might be controversial. Let me rate these probabilities into three categories: Unlikely, Possible, and Likely.

And let me divide the next 50 years into three sets of 15 years, with each set roughly comprising three elections or so.

We can, therefore, create a matrix for the scenarios:

1.   **Status Quo Scenario:**
First 15 years: Possible
Second 15 years: Unlikely
Third 15 years: Unlikely

2.   **Dominant Party Scenario:**
First 15 years: Likely
Second 15 years: Possible
Third 15 years: Possible

3.   **Two-Party Pendulum Scenario:**
First 15 years: Unlikely
Second 15 years: Possible
Third 15 years: Likely

This is my pretence at trying to be a political scientist because only when you create tables do you have some legitimacy as a political scientist; otherwise, I wouldn't have done this.

Basically, what does this say? All these scenarios foresee that the PAP will face a challenge to retain the same degree of control over Parliament as it has had in the past. So long as the very popular current PM Lee Hsien Loong remains in control — not only as PM but as Senior Minister (SM) or Minister Mentor (MM) like his predecessors, the mantle of legitimacy can be extended to younger leaders. But even Mr Lee, and I mean Mr Lee Hsien Loong, will be in his 80's by three more elections. The challenge will then be considerable from then on.

This is not actually a radical conclusion — almost everyone I informally surveyed agreed with it broadly, but differed in their estimation as to how many years it would take before the PAP would lose an election, and how many terms it would stay out of power before bouncing back. Because history also shows that most founding parties, after they lose, undergoes a period of drastic reform, and bounce back.

In fact, Mr Lee Kuan Yew himself had publicly pointed out that the PAP will eventually lose an election, but he did not foresee a date or a cause. It was in fact, to mitigate what he considered the risks involved with this inevitable event — which he dubbed a "freak" election — that the Elected Presidency was created. But as the last Presidential election showed, this controversial measure may well backfire and simply prove that the law of unintended consequences is actually very powerful.

A so-called "freak" presidential election — meaning unexpected by and unfavourable to the PAP — may happen sooner than a so-called "freak" *parliamentary* election. Another controversial measure, the creation of Group Representation Constituencies (GRCs) to require a minority-race MP in each GRC, but which has been criticised as also a convenient hurdle for opposition parties to win in GRCs, may also backfire.

So, my conclusion is that, I think measures to mitigate more so-called freak elections will not be forthcoming.

Causes for Loss of Power

So far, historical trends elsewhere point towards an election loss by the PAP in the second half of the next 50 years. Or to put it another way, it would be extraordinary if that did not happen. The issue we should now consider is: what might cause the PAP to lose a general election, given its current overwhelming dominance?

There are, in my view, three basic possibilities: first, an accidental or freak election. Second, a split within the PAP resulting in a loss to an opposition party which might not otherwise be stronger than a united PAP. And third, an anticipated, outright loss to an opposition party.

Freak Election

Advocates of the freak election thesis note that the near-absolute control of Parliament by the PAP is not reflected in the total anti-PAP votes in every general election, which has averaged between 35% to 40%.

This has been due to the first-past-the-post Westminster system which intentionally favours a strong ruling party rather than multi-party coalition governments. And so a party winning only say 60% of the total votes cast in an election may control some 90% of Parliament — as is the situation in Singapore.

However, this can also give the PAP and its supporters a false sense of security. If sufficient voters want more opposition Parliamentarians than the paltry 10% at present, or are unhappy about a particular policy, but do not necessarily want a change of government, this might result in a relatively small swing in the total votes cast — say, 8% to 10%.

This could result in a small majority still for the PAP of say, 52% against 48% of total votes cast. But it could also result in sufficient constituencies — especially the big GRCs' — being lost, to actually tip the balance and result in an unintended loss of power by the PAP.

Split in the PAP

The second cause of a loss of power would be if the PAP split into two. History shows that internal differences must be extremely severe to split a ruling party, because opposing factions are self-serving enough to thoroughly dislike each other but remain unhappily married in order to remain in power. Japan's Liberal Democratic Party (LDP) is an example of convenient marriages between extremely divergent factions.

Currently there are not any foreseeable issues nor distinct ideological rifts which can be so controversial as to cause a split. Over the long course of history, perhaps a re-unification with Malaysia, or a complete end to National Service, might qualify as fundamentally radical enough to split a party, but these sorts of issues aren't on the cards. It is hard to imagine issues of the scale of say, Scottish independence or Hong Kong's system of elections, on the Singapore horizon.

Recent issues which did not have a consensus within the PAP or Cabinet, such as granting casino licenses, or legalising gay sex, are hardly divisive enough to cause a split in a party which has prided itself in being a broad church and upholding pragmatism as its operational philosophy.

Nevertheless, the last elections have shown that retired PAP MPs do not necessarily toe the party line, and with each passing election, challenges to current leadership by current or past MPs and ministers may well grow, without the overwhelming authority of Mr Lee Kuan Yew to squash dissenting voices. In itself, the PAP now is becoming a more pluralistic party with a greater diversity of voices in its ranks, which of course is no bad thing, but carries along its own dangers.

Massive Loss of Legitimacy

The third possibility, that of an outright, convincing and even widely anticipated win by an opposition party — such as the one that occurred recently in the Indian general elections — is only possible if there is a long, irrecoverable and *massive* loss of legitimacy by the ruling party.

This is not likely to happen just because of honest policy mishaps, perhaps partly due to an innate Asian conservatism towards regime change and an Asian deference to authority. On the flip side, however, Asian electorates are increasingly intolerant about corruption in public office, partly because it is so prevalent.

China's President Xi Jinping is keenly aware of this. Widespread corruption, and not the demand for democracy or unhappiness with specific policies, will lead to the demise of the Chinese Communist Party through its total loss of legitimacy. Singapore achieved its unrivalled, enviable record of incorruptibility largely because Mr Lee Kuan Yew set a

Singapore remains exemplary among its neighbours and even its counterparts in developed countries, for its low level of corruption.

tone of governance which equated to an almost ascetic personal lifestyle. His colleague Dr Goh Keng Swee even referred to the PAP as a priesthood, a calling which involved deep personal sacrifices.

And so, its exceptionalism on incorruptibility has allowed the PAP to get away with governance styles — the paternalism of the so-called nanny state — which might be resented by many Singaporeans, but accepted because of widespread trust that whatever its policy mishaps, the political leadership is generally acting in the best interests of the public, and never for their own personal financial gains.

The question here is whether that same exceptionalism can be maintained two, three decades from now when the priesthood which was the original PAP becomes but a quaint footnote in history books, and the party starts to resemble, as many ageing political parties, a clubby, well-paid, fraternity with its own sense of entitlement.

If future political leaders become blasé about corruption, accepting it perhaps as part of the general cynicism of the New Normal, and value their occupation as similar to the well-paid investment bankers against whom their pay is benchmarked, rather than as an almost sacred mission, as Dr Goh described it, then Singapore indeed will no longer be exceptional.

And if Singaporeans become cynical about the absolute incorruptibility of their government and see their leadership as being no different than counterparts in ASEAN, in Hong Kong or Taiwan, or indeed in India and China, then the calculus of governance will change forever.

There is no evidence that corruption has increased in Singapore's public life, despite a few scandals involving mid-level bureaucrats. Singapore remains exemplary among its neighbours and even its counterparts in developed countries, for its low level of corruption. The high salaries paid to ministers will certainly mitigate the *need* for corruption, although, as we have seen with convicted investment bankers, being ultra-rich can breed an "entitlement" mentality that "more should be mine".

But generally, massive loss of trust in the PAP is not likely to happen soon, although there is certainly some cynicism about the selflessness of highly paid ministers which did not apply to the founding generation of leaders.

A slow erosion of confidence and trust towards political leadership, such as now widely exists in Western liberal democracies. Over a period of time, this gradual erosion of trust, can be as corrosive as more dramatic causes.

One of the reasons why Hong Kong youth have reacted so fiercely to the universal suffrage issue is because their Chief Executives and deputies have lost the trust of ordinary people since 1997. If the Chief Executives were appointed by Beijing but did not represent only the interests of the rich, and were not tainted by corruption, I daresay that the issue of nominated candidates would be less controversial today. Lack of democracy and authoritarianism can be grudgingly accepted if leaders have integrity and the public interest truly at heart.

Of these three possible causes for loss of power, which have the greatest likelihood of occurring? I would rate the first possibility — a freak election — as having the highest chance, followed by an internal split, and the least likely is an outright, widely predicted loss. But this is a quite arbitrary stab in the dark.

In all likelihood, it is the interplay and combination of these three scenarios in different ways, which will pose a challenge for the PAP and its scenario-planners in future decades.

Now, just as I've highlighted three possible causes for loss of power, there are many factors which can either delay or accelerate these possible causes.

One is demography. Singapore is one of the fastest-ageing nations in the world. Old people are inherently more risk-averse than the young. They want to conserve whatever they already have — be it wealth, health, or benefits.

They are not likely to risk what they have for the sake of vague idealistic notions such as freedom of speech or more opposition in Parliament.

However, the silver vote can also be vociferous about protecting their own rights. Just before the last general elections, an Institute of Policy Studies (IPS) survey showed that the percentage of elderly swing voters rose to 45.4%, compared to only 35.2% in the previous election. The only demonstrations at Hong Lim Park which have been attended by people over 60, were those protesting about Central Provident Fund (CPF) and Medisave issues.

Keenly aware of their disgruntlement, the government has since launched many initiatives to recognise this so-called Pioneer generation, including a S$ 8 billion health care package. It will be interesting to see how this translates into votes.

Another factor which could delay or accelerate the PAP's loss of power, is the PAP's organisational structure. The cadre system, found both in the Catholic Church and in communist parties, mitigates against internal fractures. As the joke goes, Lenin was in fact a closet Catholic because he admired and copied the world's most self-perpetuating system whereby the Pope chooses the cardinals who choose the Pope, and together they control hundreds of millions of people. It is, therefore, virtually impossible for upstart rebels within the Catholic Church, or in a Leninist, cadre-style political party to seize control of the party or church. Nevertheless, this can also lead to internal rigidity and intrigues.

Yet another factor is possible loss of economic competitiveness. The trade-off in fast-growth, low-freedom societies is that the delivery of a rapidly improving material life will offset the relative paucity of civil rights.

But as Singapore's economy matures and the low-hanging fruits of economic growth have all been plucked, then the economic trade-offs begin to fray, and the social compact can begin to unwind.

A final but important factor is the relative strength of opposition parties. Other than a freak election, a change of power can only happen if the electorate believes that if given the chance, an opposition party can actually govern. Recent elections have established the credibility of some opposition parties as serious-minded, competent, and constructive. The frequently made assertion that Singapore's talent pool is too small to ever have more than one credible political party, is actually quickly losing credibility.

There are also signs that the electorate is distinguishing between different opposition parties in their credibility and a sorting out process will result in only one or two strong opposition parties. One watershed event was the January 2013 by-election in Punggol East where a three-cornered fight with two opposition parties and the PAP contesting should have resulted in a PAP victory. But the Workers' Party (WP) candidate won, largely because the anti-PAP voters all cast their votes for this single party which they deemed most credible, and there was no splitting of opposition votes.

The WP is likely to be the biggest beneficiary from the next elections. If and when it wins enough seats to be considered an entrenched party — there is no hard and fast rule, but perhaps 20% of Parliamentary seats or 15 to 20 opposition MPs will make it such, it will find the going both harder and easier.

Harder, on one front because the underdog effect which cushioned it from scrutiny on various levels, will be eroded considerably. It will have to demonstrate that beyond a credible policy manifesto, it must have the organisational depth and cohesion to run a country.

Easier, because it will have more organisational resources and perhaps even a geographic stronghold from which to expand. And it can argue that competent management of town councils is a stepping stone to running a city-state.

Though ideological and policy points of difference are important, the ultimate hurdle in the leap from credible opposition to possible ruling party in the eyes of ordinary, mainly swing voters, is the ability to govern. If the opposition became the ruling party, will the proverbial trains still run on time? Will my daily life become more, or less, of a hassle than before?

Focussing on the WP's ability, or lack of it thereof, to manage the town councils in their constituencies, will be a PAP election strategy. It may also be why the WP is relatively quiet in Parliament, preferring to prove itself on the ground through rigorous door-to-door canvassing and mundane, but important constituency work. And it may also not be accidental that a special body under the PM's office was recently created to co-ordinate municipal services, recognising its electoral significance in the coming elections.

Grassroots politics will again, as in the PAP's early years, become more important, when the opposition sets up rival community organisations in its own geographic strongholds. This may permeate into the larger civil society.

One possible negative impact may be greater polarisation, but it will be offset by the positive impact of genuine grassroots leadership being tested on both sides and more of a bottom-up rather than top-down process of leadership renewal.

Having covered the politics part of this lecture, let me now talk a bit about governance. A key issue here is governability — to what extent will Singapore be more difficult to govern, regardless of whom is the ruling party?

I can identify several trends which will affect governability:

First, the ability of governments to control information will continue to erode, despite sometimes frantic and illogical attempts to stem it. Because knowledge is power, and the ability to control access to information is the key to power, governments instinctively want to be the gatekeepers of information. But, as everyone knows, increasingly, social media and its incredible variety of means for people to connect even across a heavily censored internet system, is undermining government's ability to shape how people think.

Anything censored is still widely available in alternative media, and therein lies the rub: at what point will control and censorship of the main-stream news, cultural, and entertainment media, pseudo-documentaries become counter-productive by not really achieving the purpose of blocking access to information, but instead, end up alienating the social activists who, despite their small size, and their not being heartlanders, are influencers beyond their numbers?

The Singapore government has a counter-argument and it is that even if a control or censorship measure does not achieve its stated purpose, it signals the values of a society and must be enacted irrespective of the chances for success. And this was one of the reasons advanced for our continuing to try to block pornography sites: that even if it is not going to be successful, it signals the values of a society.

So against this backdrop we now have gay penguins singing To Singapore with Love, and more of this will happen in future.

Second, it will be increasingly difficult to hold the political centre together in the midst of polarising extremes — liberals vs conservatives; local vs foreign; pro-life vs pro-abortion; gay versus straight, and so forth. Whilst fault lines along race and religion have been contained and have still not cracked, the so-called culture wars are intensifying.

The PAP government has steered clear of siding with any particular viewpoint and this moderate, centrist approach has been largely successful. But as the culture wars escalate, the government may well have to take a stance and offend at least one part of the electorate. But culture wars in themselves may not be a bad thing if seen as necessary growing pains towards what seems to be an oxymoron but in fact is a desirable goal, and that is cohesive diversity. We even see within the Catholic Church itself, the top leadership, meaning the Pope, having to stimulate discussions on what were previously totally taboo subjects.

Thirdly, diminution in the stature of political leadership will encourage the rise of so-called "non-constructive" politics. Future leaders simply cannot command the sufficient respect and moral authority to just decree what is acceptable and unacceptable criticisms. To have the authority to simply deride wide swathes of criticisms as simply non-constructive is going to be wishful thinking because people in the future are just not going to accept it.

However, if political power in Singapore will increasingly be shared between competing groups, as it is now in Hong Kong and Taiwan, it is important that political discourse does not descend to the theatrical farces which now characterise their legislative meetings. In these countries, a political culture of mutual respect has not been established. It is imperative that this be established in Singapore in the coming years, so that by common consent of all political players — rather than by ministerial decree — a consensual culture of constructive politics emerges.

Fourth, maintaining an ethos of egalitarianism in an increasingly unequal society will require more than just political oratory. Whilst Singapore was never a socialist state, its ethos was fervently egalitarian and this helped to create a sense of common purpose, exemplified by the 1970's concept of a Rugged Society, which some of us in our 60s might remember, which today sounds quaintly outdated today but did indeed embody a particular ethos.

In recent years, the ostentatious pursuit of wealth rivalling Hong Kong standards has become fashionable. Extolling our casinos, Formula 1 Grand Prix, and highest per capita number of billionaires and Lamborghinis in the world, is evidence that Singapore has now become a world class city, such exhortations, such claims to fame, could perhaps be dismissed as the crassness of the rich, except that this ethos of the elite is occurring just when income inequality has become the worst since independence.

The gulf between rich and poor Singaporeans, not only in terms of wealth but also in terms of values, is probably more than ever before, and continuing to widen.

Even the gap between old money and its sense of responsible philanthropy, and the nouveau riche's penchant for affectation and bling, is widening. So besides the sheer economic impact of income inequality, the ethos of egalitarianism is also unwinding very rapidly.

Finally, the absence of a galvanising national mission and a sense of dogged exceptionalism that we are the little dot that refuses to be smudged out, that disappearance of this dogged exceptionalism as we grow increasingly rich and complacent, it will lead to a sense of anomie — which has been defined as "personal unrest, alienation and anxiety that comes from a lack of purpose or ideals". Sociologists will tell you about the sense of anomie within a society. This is the disease of affluence which affects individual people as well as societies. And will we discover, we have arrived, only to find ourselves lost again?

If this seems unnecessarily pessimistic, it is because I personally think the danger of hubris right now is greater than the danger of under-confidence.

A discussion of Singapore politics would not be complete without touching on a major player in political governance: the civil service, or more accurately its *crème de la crème*, the elite administrative service.

There has historically been a close association between the admin service and the government, not simply because the civil service has known only one political master in 50 years, but mainly because a large number of Cabinet ministers came from the admin service.

This has led, on the positive side, to a very close and sometimes seamless relationship between the government and civil service, which is not seen anywhere else in liberal democracies with their changing ruling parties and a clear distinction between the starting and ending points of a political versus public sector career.

The negative side which has been most mentioned is the lack of intellectual and experiential diversity between the political and public sector elites, resulting in group-think and an uniformity of perspectives. This ultimately leads, it is argued, to a lack of creativity in solutions to problems, a blinkered view of the world and how people will react to policies, and a lack of robustness in policy debates.

A new dimension which may be emerging is the impact of the New Normal, with its increasing uncertainties over the electoral performance of the PAP in successive general elections, on the civil service. A civil service whose identity has been so closely tied to the fortunes of the ruling party can become demoralised and disoriented if the ruling party is increasingly uncertain of its own future.

With more electoral volatility in the future, it is imperative that the civil service work harder to develop its own sense of self, its own ethos and values. The purpose is not just to distance itself from the ruling party, but to develop a culture and identity strong, robust and resilient enough to embrace and absorb, and not become divided and uncertain, should more young civil servants hold opposing views from the ruling party. A politicised civil service would be disastrous for Singapore should the politics of the New Normal intensify in coming decades.

My final remarks are about today's younger generation, the inheritors of the future.

Fifty years is both a very long and a very short time. In this period, Singapore has moved from Third World to First World, with physical and economic changes beyond recognition. But there is a real danger that we may in reality become stuck in a kind of First World-minus, with First World economic characteristics but without the socio-political or socio-cultural attributes — what our leaders call "heartware" — which characterises a deeper, more holistic maturity.

And yet 50 years in the lifetime of a family or even an individual is not all that long. Three generations: my parents, myself, and my children — have all lived through parts of this 50 years. Shared experiences and common memories still bind people across five decades.

The deepening of a shared national identity, the pursuit of a compelling social vision, and the shaping, articulation, and moulding of that vision through a collective imagination, is the central task of the younger generation. Stumbling into the future without a clue as to what you want, and what are the promises and the perils, is quite possibly the best way to ensure that we will encounter an accidental disaster.

> **There is a real danger that we may in reality become stuck in a kind of First World-minus, with First World economic characteristics but without the socio-political or socio-cultural attributes.**

Thankfully I have not, in my conversations with young people, encountered either the hubris or the immobilising self-doubts which I was afraid of. It is not as if the young people I spoke to were very happy with the state of affairs in Singapore today. Far from it. Almost everyone was critical of one issue or another, and to varying degrees.

But what impressed me was the overwhelming sense of what sociologists call self-agency — the simple notion that I can change things; that I am in control of my life and my future.

As someone who has been somewhat depressed by the tired cynicism of my own peers, I found this boundless optimism — some would call it the naïveté of youth — tremendously encouraging. Our young people are not apathetic nor are they sycophants — but they take the society they live in today as a given, a matter-of-fact reality for which they neither feel the same degrees of gratitude or resentment as members of my generation.

They have also broadened their vision of "Singapore My Home" to be more than just relentless but uni-dimensional economic progress, to include other aspirations. The thoughtful young Singaporean today recognises that the vision of a future Singapore cannot simply be a top-down narrative, but will have to be co-created from the ground up.

They regard the government and the PAP as a matter of fact — not a saviour, nor a tyrant, but somewhat like a parent who is respected but who must be grown out of. Clearly, a paternalistic political culture is not going to excite, much less retain, the loyalty of younger Singaporeans.

Whereas in my generation the government and the PAP were always the reference point around which all discussion revolved, whether positive or critical, today's young people seem to be bored by too much purely political discussion. They want to move on, to talk about: *what next*? And what next means a myriad of civil society causes, sometimes similar, sometimes overlapping, sometimes even opposing and contradictory causes.

What unites them all is the immediacy of self-agency; not waiting around for somebody else to do something you think is needed, but doing it yourself. This kind of political DIY or Do-It-Yourself attitude has, I believe, in the past decade encouraged a participatory democracy which actually resembles Singapore's early years, but which then surrendered to a long period of developmental authoritarianism during perhaps my growing up years.

One striking example — which was not imaginable in my generation — was the response to the famous Gay Penguins episode — which will go down in Singapore's history, I hope, as the kind of comic relief we need as a nation whilst we tackle the underlying big issues.

The fact that some bureaucrats banned some children's books as pro-gay and anti-family is not unexpected, and not dis-similar in logic to the banning of chewing gum or long hair decades earlier.

But twenty years ago, such bureaucratic actions — not necessarily about LGBT issues but about anything else, would have been met only by grudging acquiescence.

But as a sign of the times, including the power of social media, the response this time was some 400 young parents decamping to the national library to read the banned and to-be-pulped books to their children. It was not a strident political demonstration, and more like a children's outing. But the point was clear.

And the same is true for the unprecedented 26,000 people who gathered at the Pink Dot event — not just to celebrate gay rights nor to oppose the government, but to celebrate the increasing diversity and self-agency of civil society.

So I conclude today's talk with a hopeful view of Singapore politics in the next 50 years, simply because in the larger picture, I do not see the ossification of an ageing political elite increasingly out of touch with a restless youth, such as led to the Arab Spring; nor do I see fundamentally divisive issues such as in Hong Kong over its relationship with China; nor the exhaustion of Old Europe unable and unwilling to confront big, difficult issues.

At 50, Singapore is still a young nation in search of its own future. I do not think there are more, or fewer, challenges ahead than in the past 50 years. They will simply be different challenges. It will be the task of subsequent S R Nathan Fellows to continue identifying and debating them, and I hope I have set the ball rolling.

I just want to add an end-note to this lecture. A few weeks ago my wife and I visited the British Museum's latest exhibition in London, entitled "Ming: 50 years that changed China". This period from 1400 to 1450 saw an unprecedented flowering of Chinese civilisation in the arts, diplomacy and trade. It was perhaps best exemplified not by its emperors, but the Muslim eunuch Zheng He.

His armada of ships with over 20,000 people on each voyage and on ships ten times larger than any of its European contemporaries, travelled to all corners of the world a century before Columbus and Vasco da Gama. But the point was not that.

The point was what the curators noted in that exhibition — that this golden period of Chinese civilisation coincided with or was in fact caused by, a pro-active philosophy of ethnic, religious, intellectual tolerance, an intentional cultivation of diversity, and a purposeful curiosity to know the unknown. In subsequent dynasties, the closing of the Chinese mind led to centuries of darkness and humiliation which are only now ending.

The moral for Singapore is two-fold: first, that 50 years is a long enough time for a people to create wonders and so we should see the next 50 years with an excitement towards what Singapore can yet become, and with a childlike amazement at each unfolding opportunity. And second, that openness, tolerance, and diversity, whilst also bringing their own risks, are the essential ingredients for greatness — a goal which is not beyond our collective grasp.

Questions and Answers
Moderator: Janadas Devan

Question: My question is on public institutions such as the People's Association (PA) and Housing & Development Board (HDB). People feel that the civil service may be in some sense too politicised or too used to a certain ruling party. For the long term sustainability of our system, we should have public institutions to be seen to be neutral and fair. What are your comments to this?

Ho Kwon Ping (HKP): I understand your question to be: will ostensibly public institutions that are meant to serve the entire public good and the entire nation, possibly be utilised for the interests of a particular political party? Cases we've seen include HDB upgrading applying only to those constituencies that have only voted for the government and so on. Is that correct? I think what is going to happen is what normally happens in any country where you begin to have a greater balance of power. It is not entirely unnatural for a ruling political party that has a huge dominance to conveniently utilise whatever instruments of state that are available to it for its own benefit. It's understandable, as long as it's legal.

However, if you begin to see a greater balance of power in Parliament, I think that voice would be strong enough that the instruments of state and civil servants will probably have to recognise that they have to toe the line and have to really be completely neutral. It behooves the civil service to recognise that such things may be coming, and that you may even have younger members of the civil service who might have opposing views from older people. It's critical for the civil service to not become politicised.

Question: What would happen if indeed in a super freak election, The Workers' Party came into power? Would the government allow this? Meaning to say, would they accept it? Or will there be an unprecedented military takeover?

HKP: I do believe that the ruling party would accept it because this ruling party, I think, plays by the rules although they push them a little bit.

The ruling party understands history, and it well recognises as I have pointed out that virtually all ruling founding parties that lost the election got voted back in again. This ruling party is wise enough to recognise that losing one election and biding its time to win back again, is quite easily achievable but disallowing the democratic process to proceed is going to destroy Singapore.

Question: Singapore society has changed, and the young people feel empowered. I think they want to be governed with a lighter touch than your generation and mine. In view of this, do you think the decision by the Media Development Authority recently to ban To Singapore, With Love, is not in keeping with the kind of light touch governance that we expect to see?

HKP: I felt this was a missed opportunity on the part of the government. I haven't seen the movie, I only saw snippets on YouTube. The snippets were of really aged people in Thailand and elsewhere who might have posed a threat to the Singapore government in the past, but are quite different people today.

My sense is that the government should not have banned it but should have welcomed it and screened it, and used it as an opportunity to educate Singaporeans that there was a hard ruthless struggle for the soul of Singapore. Some people won, some people lost. Those who lost are not to be treated badly, they believed in what they sought to do.

But most importantly, the sense I think any Singaporean would have if they have watched that movie, is the same sense when our government many years ago allowed us to go to China again.

Remember for many years they did not allow us to go to China because they thought we would then be duped by the communists. What happened instead is that we went to China and sensed an empathy for Chinese culture, but when we came back to Singapore, we were ultra grateful for the society we live in.

The exiles are not terrible people. They believed in their cause but we younger Singaporeans understand that it is so fortunate that the PAP won.

Because the system that we live under today, for all its flaws, is a much better system today than the system that would exist if they had won. It would have been a system of Cuba, it would have been Vietnam.

But at the same time, are Singaporeans not educated, matured enough to recognise that the battle for the soul of Singapore was won by the people who should have won and they won, and be magnanimous enough to let this be a teaching exercise?

Banning the film on the grounds of it being self-serving means that we have to postpone the period of education and of history being told from another perspective. When these historical issues are re-examined, history will come to the conclusion that the battle was won by those who should have won and the government need not write every line and chapter of history. Let there be enough room for others who may be self-serving to say their piece. The film could have helped to illustrate the reality of what the PAP went through and how they made the right decision. The battle that Lee Kuan Yew had to fight was a real battle with real people that is not just in history books.

Question: Is rising income disparity a good thing overall for Singapore in the next 50 years? Does it make people hungrier?

HKP: If you want to be more technical about it, income inequality always exists in a capitalist society. Income inequality is positive to the extent that it is an incentive for people to do better. So income inequality by itself is not necessarily a good or bad thing, it is a simple fact. Measurements of income inequality are also quite hugely distorted in a society like Singapore. You just need Eduardo Saverin and a few other Facebook billionaires to relocate here and bingo, our per capita GDP and our income inequality and our gini coefficient change.

Two points are important: First, that income inequality at the lower end of the socio-economic strata, at the broad base level, does not increase more. We had that happening here — this happens everywhere in the developed world. With the digital age and the information-based society, those with lower skills tend to be left behind. A lot of job destruction is happening right now all over the world, and that is leading to income inequality which any responsible government has to try and mitigate by educating the people who are left behind to higher skill levels and so on.

Second, that our ethos of egalitarianism continues. Because even if I earn less than you, so long as I feel equal to you, so long as you treat me with the same amount of respect, we can have income inequality, but we can have an egalitarian society. That is very different from a communist system where we are all essentially equal. Pure absolute income inequality will always persist. But if it is coupled with inegalitarianism, with people flaunting wealth — things we had in Singapore's early years which we've moved away from — we are going to see more social problems and social tensions arise.

Question: What defines political legitimacy in Singapore? Do you think the Singapore electorate uses their vote to signal how they want policymaking to progress or as a reward for past performance?

HKP: Broadly speaking, I think it is both generational and demographic. Younger people are more likely to vote for policies — they vote for their future. Older people, who have more to lose, will basically vote to reward a government for what they've been given, and younger, more idealistic, people would vote for what the government promises to do, broadly speaking.

On legitimacy — it is when people recognise that the leadership that is there — whether it is appointed like the Communist Party, whether it is elected as in Singapore, or quasi-elected as in Hong Kong — might make policy mishaps but are trusted to be in their roles for the sake of the people they are supposed to lead. Legitimacy is conferred upon leaders whom people see are truly acting in their best interests.

Question: You mentioned that you have spoken to young people, and they want to participate in a more pluralistic society. How do they want to participate?

HKP: I can only talk about the young people that my children are kind enough to arrange for me to meet, otherwise I wouldn't have all the opportunities to meet young people. I would contrast them with my generation. In my generation, we generally sat around and griped. We would criticise the government on all measures, or some people would be audacious enough to go and run in a political party for instance. But because the government was so over-dominant, it basically did all the good things in which you just sat back and enjoyed it, or they did all the things you didn't like and you would criticise them; it was those two extremes.

Young people today are less concerned about the government being the centre of everything against which they either complain or they love. It is there, it is a presence, but they have a sense of self-agency. They do things to express their views, as happened with the Pink Dot event, as happened with the protest against the National Library Board removing children's books which showed alternative family structures. These actions would not have happened in my time, because they were not partisan political events. They were not in support of a particular political party. They were just young people saying "I don't agree with this", or in the case of Pink Dot, "I celebrate diversity".

People just go out now and do what they want to do to express themselves. This sense of self-agency is much stronger now among young people and that gives me hope for the future of Singapore.

LECTURE II

ECONOMY AND BUSINESS

G ood evening and welcome to the second lecture in the IPS-Nathan Lectures series, which will deal with the Singapore economy in the next 50 years.

Economists can overlay standard boom-to-bust business cycles on traditional forecasts, and extrapolate currently foreseeable trends into different scenarios where long term means 10 years. This is dealing with known knowns and accounts for perhaps up to 90% of forecasting models.

Then there is the crystal-ball gazing bordering on futurology, with notions like artificial intelligence, space travel, stem cell organ regeneration, global viral epidemics, Armageddon-like climate change, and umpteen other neat stuff in the realm of science fiction movies. These are unknown unknowns.

In between is the biggest challenge for think-tank tenants or wanna-be academic fellows like me: that's the realm of the known unknowns, a nether-world between predictive forecasting and irresponsible speculation, where perhaps the probability of events occurring is a pretty even 50:50.

The biggest known unknown facing us in the next 50 years, is figuring out the impact to Singapore of what is already clearly going to be the most disruptive economic change in the past two hundred years.

That event can be summarised by a very short quote in the *Economist*[1] magazine:

> *"The modern digital revolution — with its hallmarks of computer power, connectivity, and data ubiquity... is disrupting and dividing the world of work on a scale not seen for more than a century. Vast wealth is being created without many workers, and for all but an elite few, work no longer guarantees a rising income."*

It is like a massive tsunami originating in the middle of the ocean and hurtling towards all coastal countries. How it will impact each country is still unknown, but every country that sees the tsunami coming towards it, better be prepared.

We do know from history, that every technological disruption displaces some jobs but after a short, painful transition, it creates more jobs by either increasing consumer power or, through ancillary employment from the initial technology, it enables everyone to be better off.

Lower-productivity jobs and lower value-added enterprises give way to those higher on the skills and value-added ladder, in an ongoing process which the economist Joseph Schumpeter called "creative destruction". This is a concept that I think most of us are familiar with.

We went through this once in the mid-1980's and we are right in the middle of another economic restructuring now.

But, is it different this time round? What is alarming governments and academics alike is that the pace of the digital revolution is so fast that it is displacing workers in far larger numbers than before, across the entire spectrum of the economy; and in a supreme irony, rendering some low-paid jobs more viable than higher-skilled ones.

Previous technological change was linear in speed; digital disruption is exponential in acceleration. Previous technological change automated manual work; digital change

Previous technological change was linear in speed; digital disruption is exponential in acceleration.

---

[1] http://eresources.nlb.gov.sg/newspapers/Digitised/Article/straitstimes 19740913-1.2.104.aspx

automates both cognitive and manual work. Any kind of routinised work, even of high cognitive order, can be done by computers, robotics and artificial intelligence. Ironically, the job of the office cleaner is more assured than that of the insurance claim adjuster or IT call centre consultant, both back-office jobs which may require university degrees but are routinised.

The job-destroying power of the digital revolution is frightening: a recent Oxford University study analysed 700 occupations and concluded that 47% can be computerised and gotten rid of. Another study projects that up to half of the types of jobs available today will have been destroyed in ten years.

Singapore is particularly exposed to the digital revolution, with our disproportionately high dependence, compared to other ASEAN economies, on foreign MNC's engaged in precisely those businesses which can be digitally disrupted. Government is exhorting everyone to increase our productivity to justify higher wages, but the danger is that automation may leapfrog us and render that higher skilled job obsolete before we've trained the worker — or more ominously, ourselves.

Labour markets are hollowing out and polarising highest skilled and lowest skilled jobs, with very little employment in the middle. This known unknown is one of the biggest challenges for Singapore in the next half-century, not only in terms of its ramifications for employment but also worsening income inequality. I saw a clipping in the TODAY newspaper where it talked about the so-called unhappiness of Singapore workers. What was most interesting was that the occupations where people were most unhappy were the people working in MNCs, banks and in precisely those businesses which are in the middle of being disrupted. And they found that in fact the lower skilled occupations had a higher happiness index, and I wonder whether we are beginning to see the impact of this change.

I will ask two questions of our known unknowns:

First, has the strategy which enabled Singapore to rise from Third to First World in one generation run out of steam in the New Economy and must be radically altered or even replaced? For example, does the digital economy dictate that hitherto key economic pillars such as manufacturing, be replaced by a pure services economy?

Second, what adjustments to the fundamentals of our strategy may be required in the light of known unknowns?

Section One — The Strategy

The Three Ls

Let me turn to my first question, that of strategy. Singapore is the only fully sovereign and independent nation with such disproportion between its land mass and population size: like a dwarf with an oversized head. Monaco, Liechtenstein, Macau, and even Hong Kong — itself double the size of Singapore — don't count, as they are essentially protectorates with no sovereign foreign policy nor military capability, nor broad economic capabilities.

And yet, despite the absence of a hinterland, Singapore has chosen a path of economic development which is unprecedented elsewhere. And that is to replicate a comprehensively multi-sectoral, developed economy comprising different manufacturing industries as well as different service sectors, on a land mass marginally larger than the resort island of Phuket and with a total GDP larger than Malaysia with a population four times larger.

I suppose that is the power of necessity. What Singapore's leaders did immediately upon an independence more thrust upon them than actually desired, was to embark on what I will call the "Three L's Strategy":

- First, Location: Building upon Singapore's historic choke point between East Asia and Europe to ensure that it remained the maritime trading centre between these two worlds, and then leveraging off its location to be the regional aviation hub and finance centre.
- Second, Land: Intentional intervention against free-market principles for allocation of scarce land to achieve very purposeful and targeted national objectives, ranging from affordable public housing to industrial estates for foreign manufacturers.
- Third, Labour: Liberal policy towards foreign workers to keep costs low, while continually upgrading skills and productivity of Singaporeans to ensure competitiveness against neighbouring countries.

What are the threats to each of the three "L"s of the strategy, and what are the possible responses?

The First L — Location

Is our hub status declining into irrelevance as global trends create new hubs or even renders the whole notion obsolete? Climate change has opened a year-round, ice-free Arctic passage between the massive economies of Northeast Asia and Europe which may eventually bypass Singapore.

Massive investments in rail and road networks will allow every part of China to access ports in the Indian Ocean, or carry cargo across Russia and Central Asia to Europe directly, without passing through the Straits of Malacca.

Changi Airport and Singapore Airlines are challenged by the rise of Middle Eastern airports and airlines, which have siphoned away much of the so-called Kangaroo route between the UK and Australia. And the rise of numerous world-class airports in China has resulted in direct flights between the rest of the world and Chinese cities, bypassing Singapore.

Another hub-based business activity is financial services. The rise of China has created a strong Northeast Asian financial cluster comprising Shanghai, Hong Kong, Tokyo and Seoul. Further westwards, Dubai, Doha, and Abu Dhabi effectively service South and Central Asia, and Africa. And with Sydney servicing Australasia, Singapore remains as the financial services centre for only Southeast Asia.

But even that circle is shrinking: Bangkok will be the center for Myanmar and the Indochina of old: Vietnam, Laos, Cambodia. With Indonesia's new-found dynamism and confidence, will Jakarta still see Singapore as its New York or develop its own?

Certainly, if capital markets are anything to go by, Singapore's Stock Exchange has in the past decade fallen considerably behind other centres like Hong Kong.

These challenges will not result in any sudden and dramatic decline in Singapore's strategic role. Instead, it may be a long, slow slide. The history of Venice, always touted as the Renaissance global city which Singapore should emulate, has its less-popularised dark side.

We all know how Venice rose to be the hub of East–West trade, with its terminus of the overland Silk Road on one hand, and on the other, its maritime opening into the Mediterranean world, which was the centre of Western civilisation at that time.

What we may remember less, is how the slow decline of Venice began with new shipbuilding technologies which enabled the Atlantic-facing sea-faring nations like England, Spain, France and Portugal to discover the New World. This irrevocably led to the decline of the Mediterranean as the centre of the Western world, but it was slow enough that only backward looking historians have noticed it.

If we fast forward a few hundred years, will a similar strategic vulnerability affect Singapore? Has it already begun, but we remain happily ignorant, like the proverbial frog nonchalantly cooking to death without so much as a croak because the water temperature rises so slowly that it doesn't know it's dying, festooned with its many medals for competitiveness and being number one in this and that?

The Second L — Land

Land, are we simply running out of it despite ceaseless reclamation? And is its high cost making manufacturing so unviable that we should simply get out of it? Is it also making affordable home ownership an unachievable goal for future generations?

The two countries most similar to Singapore in size of population, are Denmark and Finland. They are also similar in gross economic output, with Denmark slightly larger and Finland slightly smaller, than Singapore. But Denmark's land mass is 60 times larger, and Finland is 485 times larger than Singapore. The term Little Red Dot, intended as an insult, is a reality.

The whole point of having a large landmass is to benefit from a symbiotic metropolis-hinterland development strategy. But Singapore is the only independent nation in the Wikipedia list of over 200 nations, with a metropolis but not the slightest hinterland. Attempts to create proxy hinterlands in Southern Johor, the Riau islands, or China, have not blossomed to become the "Growth Triangles" which they were touted to be some 10 to 15 years ago. They may be profitable ventures and attract tenants but a proxy hinterland not governed by the same set of laws or the same government, is not a true hinterland.

So, if we are running out of land, should we not focus on high value-added services and abandon a manufacturing strategy? Hong Kong and Singapore some two decades ago had roughly the same 20% percent of their GDP devoted to manufacturing. Hong Kong has abandoned manufacturing totally for the services route while Singapore on the other hand, has consistently kept manufacturing to about 20% of its economic output. Is this a misplaced commitment?

The other big issue involving land scarcity is its impact on the price of public housing. To the extent that worsening wealth inequality is a growing economic and social problem, is our land pricing policy serving the needs of our people? What indeed is the value of a rising per capita GDP if the cost of our homes per capita is rising even faster?

The Singapore housing landscape comprises three distinct markets: the Housing & Development Board (HDB) first-home market; the HDB re-sale market, and the private property market.

The globalisation of residential property ownership in recent years has driven Singapore private home prices close to London and New York levels.

The HDB re-sale market, de-regulated in the past decade to enable public housing owners to enjoy asset enhancement, has largely moved in tandem.

But the results were paradoxical. HDB owners do not feel richer as research has found. Unlike large countries with hinterlands where urban home-owners could monetise their homes and move to the city outskirts, or to say, retirement communities in scenic but inexpensive locales, Singaporeans are not able to monetise their homes unless they emigrate or downgrade — which has not been popular. And they certainly don't feel richer simply because their homes are now more valuable — economists have not detected any positive wealth effect on consumption.

This was not the case 20 years ago when home-owners could upgrade without the same cost as today. But since resale deregulation, rising home prices have only benefitted the already rich private property owners. Studies have concluded that rising prices actually channel income distribution away

> **Studies have concluded that rising prices actually channel income distribution away from own-use buyers, whether first-time or up-graders, towards developers, banks, property investors and speculators.**

from own-use buyers, whether first-time or upgraders, towards developers, banks, property investors and speculators.

As two National University of Singapore (NUS) economists Tilak Abeysinghe and Wong Yan Hao noted in a research paper,

> "it is this re-distributional aspect of rising property prices that could add to the widening income gaps".

Exactly how affordable is housing in Singapore? The 10th Demographia International Housing Affordability Survey, conducted in 2013, uses an index which takes into account the average sale price of housing versus average annual income of a household.

If housing costs exceed three times the annual household incomes, warning bells should ring. Singapore's rating of 5.1 put it in the "severely unaffordable" category, but Demographia data is not encompassing of the spectrum of housing markets here, and used only HDB resale prices and not entry-level prices for their data. Demographia has also recognised that in comparison to other metropolitan cities like Hong Kong, Vancouver, San Francisco, San Jose, Sydney, Melbourne, Auckland, and London, Singapore's results have been "stellar". Compared to Hong Kong, we would be at least three to four times more affordable. Incidentally, we are still more expensive than Tokyo and Osaka, but that might be more a reflection of how their economies have stagnated than as to how expensive we are. Very recently, the Government enhanced measures such as the Special Central Provident Fund (CPF) Housing Grant, which will help lower and middle income families buy their first subsidised home. But the whole issue of housing affordability in Singapore is not entirely clear, and it's going to be a very important issue going into the next 50 years, precisely because we are not a country with a hinterland where you can essentially move from rising prices in New York, you move to Florida, rising prices in London, you move to places outside London. There aren't many places you can move to from Singapore and with an improving economy, and with totally finite land, housing affordability is an issue.

The Third L — Labour

The same doubts plague this resource as with Land, but is more intractable because it involves human lives.

Whereas the dilemma of land scarcity is largely one of pricing and allocation priority, labour scarcity, cost, and productivity are related in complex and sometimes contradictory ways. Add in foreign versus local labour, and the issues are very intertwined.

Section Two — The Response

My second task is to identify possible changes to the Three L's of the basic strategy if it is to remain relevant for another 50 years. Let me start by saying that I believe the first L — Location — is a challenge more easily surmounted with adroit rebalancing. — The second L — Land — may require a more fundamental re-think about how to ensure home affordability, and a possible new role for the HDB, my little giraffe in the room, which I will touch on later. The third L — Labour — may justify relooking immigration and educational policies.

The First L — Location

How do we maintain our competitiveness as Singapore's strategic location declines?

I believe that the answer is in creating several critical eco-systems of business activity which are so elaborately inter-related that they cannot be reconstructed by competitors; is the result of continual incremental improvements over decades; and can stand their own in global competitiveness regardless of geography.

> I believe that the answer is in creating several critical eco-systems of business activity which are so elaborately inter-related that they cannot be reconstructed by competitors.

Let me highlight a few examples of such eco-systems which we have been building over 20 years.

Aviation is one. Changi Airport and Singapore Airlines may decline in importance. But if we add to our early start as an aviation hub, global capability in aviation leasing, financing and insurance; if we have the top engine repair and maintenance facilities here manned by very skilled technicians; if we attract the most sophisticated avionics and small precision components manufacturers here; if we create a support environment of local SMEs which can service their outsourced needs; and if we add to all that, cutting-edge research in our universities on the digital technologies related to the future of aviation …

If we do all that, there will be perhaps be only one or two other global competitors to Singapore in this domain. And it won't be Dubai, Abu Dhabi, Shanghai, or anywhere else, even though the aviation traffic going through Dubai, Abu Dhabi, Shanghai may be easily overtaking Singapore's.

The same is true in the life sciences. There are diseases more prevalent amongst East Asian racial groups, or in our climatic zones. The eco-system required to have a cutting-edge life sciences eco-system includes not only our universities but also our hospitals; it requires technicians and scientists, and a host of supporting services which again can provide opportunities to our SMEs.

And the same is also true in other knowledge-intensive, creative industries such as information and communications technology.

Even the oldest heavy industry to invest in Singapore, the petroleum refining industry, has been continually upgraded over the past decades to now include a wide range of downstream products, as well as ancillary services such as oil and gas futures trading, and even LNG storage in underground rock caverns.

The same is true for financial services, where a regional advantage some 30 years ago has been parlayed into a global leading position in wealth and funds management or forex trading, even as other purely regional advantages have declined.

This strategy is good for another 50 years, but the purposeful, deliberate selection of specific industries as the winners of tomorrow is itself risky. It requires a judicious balance between planning and market forces, and close collaboration between policymakers and industry. Another risk is the very expensive link between applied research and product development. Research funding cannot always have immediate commercial applications and yet funding cannot be open-ended; finding the right balance will again require clear, far-sighted but accurate judgement.

Finally, even should Singapore's geographic location become less strategic in a global context, the eventual creation of a genuine ASEAN Economic Community will finally provide a more homogeneous, relatively affluent market of over 700 million people for our SMEs. When I was a young journalist, I was already happily writing about a tariff-free ASEAN. Thirty years later, it still has not really happened, but 30 years from now, I presume it will finally happen. But they better move fast because every ASEAN country has its own hives of buzzing SME activity, possibly more hungry and aggressive than ours.

The Second L — Land

I had identified two challenges: viability of manufacturing in the face of land shortages, and housing affordability.

On the first challenge, there is no evidence that manufacturing of high value, sophisticated products require more space or labour than services.

In fact, it may be the other way around — the output per square meter of space or worker is probably multiple times higher in a life-sciences production plant than in a food court. The choice really is a false dichotomy if one chooses between services and manufacturing, as Hong Kong actually has found to its great detriment. Hong Kong now has a very fragile economy of, on one hand, very high-end financial services and property, and everything else below that is very low-skilled. That is the big mistake Hong Kong has made by moving out of manufacturing. The choice is not between services and manufacturing. It is between low and high valued activities of any kind.

In the new economy with its customised, on-demand production, don't think of large factories with thousands of people. You are looking now at 3-D printing of as-needed components, there will almost be no distinction between services and manufacturing. Knowledge creation leading to product creation will be a seamless process: medical research leading to drug manufacture on demand; or design and then production of nano-technology components — these are just a few examples.

The choice is not between services and manufacturing. It is between low and high valued activities of any kind.

Now, let's go on to the giraffe in the room. The second challenge of housing affordability is more intractable and perhaps requires a more radical approach. How do we become?

The research paper I quoted earlier hints at a possible way. Let me quote from their conclusion:

> "The average growth rate of lifetime income for cohorts born after 1960… has been about 4–5 per cent which has also been the average growth rate of per capita disposable income since 1975. Property prices should fall in line with this trend.
>
> Although it is difficult to avoid property price cycles, policies could be devised to reduce the amplitude of these cycles. In this regard, it is worth questioning why one should let the private housing market — that accounts only for about 20 per cent of the housing stock — to dominate the price trends of the entire housing market and erode housing affordability."

There are two critical implications from this observation. First, that property prices should perhaps be more actively managed so that they match the growth rate of lifetime income or about 4% — 5% per year.

And second, that in terms of pricing the tail should not wag the dog — public housing prices should perhaps determine private housing prices, not the other way round.

Both of these suggestions point to one possible idea: that of a national housing price regulator. Before private developers and free-market economists shout "Foul", we should realise that competition within regulated price bands is already found in other economic sectors — electricity and telecommunications, for example. More pertinent, we already have price regulation through HDB unilaterally setting the price of entry-level flats.

One objective of a national housing price regulator would be to integrate and influence the pricing of the three housing markets — HDB entry level, HDB resale, and private housing, so

In terms of pricing the tail should not wag the dog — public housing prices should perhaps determine private housing prices, not the other way round.

that the whole market is not led by private housing, which in turn is led by foreign demand. Another goal would be to have prices strike a balance between housing as an utility — the goal of young, first time owners — and housing as a wealth asset, a store of value — the goal of older owners or investors.

Singapore has never really had a totally free-market system for land utilisation or pricing anyway. It has always been subordinated to national economic or social objectives. This social-democrat orientation of our pioneer political leaders fundamentally differentiated Singapore from Hong Kong's *laissez-faire*, pro-oligopoly economy.

Affordable home ownership, our pioneer leaders fervently believed, underpinned the Singapore identity and was the bedrock of social stability. That goal must remain a paramount objective of political governance and not the dictates of the free market.

In its early years, the primary task of the new PAP government was to build massive numbers of affordable public housing in the quickest time possible. There were no private sector developers whom the government could cooperate with to undertake such a massive and ambitious programme, so HDB became the biggest housing developer in Singapore — by necessity. Fifty years on, that has not changed.

Our public housing programs today resemble that of a command economy. The only country that produces as much public housing as Singapore is North Korea. For almost 40 years until 2002, young Singaporeans essentially queued for a flat in their desired location and were allocated based on availability. This was called the Registration for Flats System (RFS).

Typical of a planned economy, supply was based on planned projections and not fluctuating market demand. When the Asian financial crisis hit in 1997, HDB was left with 20,000 empty flats which it could not unload by price discounting, as this would have infuriated those who bought at normal prices.

The RFS program was suspended and replaced by the Build-to-Order (BTO) program under which, as the name suggests, HDB blocks are built only when sufficient units are sold. That has led to an approximate four-year wait for a flat.

In 1960, HDB had a total housing stock of over 120,000 units. This figure rose rapidly and as of 2013 stood at 933,367. That probably makes it the single largest housing developer in the world, except perhaps for North Korea.

As can be expected, a planned economy for housing and a free-market economy for the rest of the country, will have contradictions. From 2002 to 2010, not enough flats were built and led to a backlog of unmet demand — with its electoral consequences.

The government then ramped up supply again and in the past two years have built an average 26,000 units per year — close to the total amount built in the four years from 2006 to 2010.

This kind of dislocation is not fundamentally different from the problems which arise when say, Chinese planners decided how much steel the country needed, or North Korea building public housing. The mismatch of supply and demand not only leads to unhappy customers with its political consequences, but also leads to distortions in the entire construction and building supplies sector, and also in the influx of foreign workers. Increasingly affluent and choosy customers are also not happy with the lack of variety which a monopoly public-housing developer can provide.

Furthermore, it is also difficult to determine who should qualify for public housing as the country becomes more affluent. The Executive Condominium (EC) scheme was introduced to satisfy the so-called "sandwich class"; the Design Build and Sell Scheme (DBSS) was a further case of mission creep.

It angered public housing users who felt that resources were being devoted to a new elite within the public housing spectrum. The scheme was short-lived and soon dropped.

It has become increasingly clear to me that there is yet another elephant in the room, with its legs in every sector of the country, from social identity to economy to family to sustainability. That elephant is the HDB.

And again, as with the PAP, its elephantine status is ironically due to its success in providing mass affordable housing — one of the true achievements in our Third to First World ascent. But its sheer dominance of the landscape by this elephant warrants some questioning as to its proper role in the Singapore of the next 50 years.

When we eventually approach our 100th anniversary in 2065, should some 80% of our housing stock still be designed and priced by one developer, whose sense of what the market wants and should pay, simply determine what we get?

In every affluent and developed society, consumer tastes have become far more complex and nuanced to be served by a single product supplier. In an extremely land-scarce economy, private sector demand — and particularly from wealthy foreigners — cannot be the price setter for the rest of the housing markets.

It may be timely for HDB to consider a gradual and phased exit over the next decades, from its role as housing developer in order to focus on a new dual role: first, as master land developer for entire new towns or districts, and second, as the regulator of housing prices in these areas, and to get out of the developer business entirely.

Some functions of the new-imagined HDB would parallel what the Urban Redevelopment Authority (URA) does as town planner, but going beyond, the HDB would be master developer also, investing in all the town infrastructure. It could even play a developmental role and invest in large-scale, low-return but labour-saving prefabrication technologies for contractors to avail themselves of.

But its most important and sensitive function could be the setting of residential product sale-price caps for each land parcel, which in turn would then be auctioned off to private developers. The competition by private developers on detailed design, quality, features and so forth would ensure that market forces dictate, but within residential price ranges set by HDB.

All housing developments will then in fact be private, with a single master land developer selling parcels to private developers.

HDB estates will also be real towns, with housing of different price ranges so as to erode the social distinctions that we still have, and should not have, between public and private housing. As with now, resales could be allowed after a holding period.

If I were to somewhat tongue-in-cheek, express the benefits of a reconstituted HDB, in traditional Chinese Communist Party style, it would be what I would call "The Five No-Mores":

1.   No more monopoly developer for public housing;
2.   No more supply and demand imbalance as the private sector will sort this out through the invisible hand, and undertake market risk;

3.   No more private versus government developers, as all housing will be undertaken by private developers, with government only regulating home unit price caps;
4.   No more social stratification or social divide based on HDB versus private housing ;
5.   No more private or foreign demand setting prices, as government can release land at lower price caps to bring down prices;

And to continue, the function of HDB will be the "Two Regulates":

1.   Regulate the supply and type of residential land
2.   Regulate the residential unit sale price ranges for land parcels, which will then be auctioned to private developers.

From a policy perspective, it would be using supply-side levers — the supply of land with caps on final product pricing — to regulate property cycles, rather than demand-side levers, which is to subdue demand through restrictions on debt financing, or taxes on purchase.

Even if one agrees in principle with the Five No Mores proposal, implementation will take decades. A pilot project may be worthwhile to throw up undiscovered issues.

But integrating the Five No-Mores model with existing HDB inventory will be difficult and it may just be easier for existing 99-year old leases to expire and then start afresh with the new model. Of course, the entire issue of what to do when leasehold land expires, is going to challenge other governments in the region with their own leasehold assets maturing.

The Third L is Labour

This is perhaps the most complex problem, ranging from job destruction and polarisation, to stagnant productivity, to over-reliance on foreign workers.

One response has been tried, has worked, but is painful. First attempted in the 1980's to ratchet the economy up the skills and wages ladder through a forced squeezing on the supply of foreign labour coupled with economy-wide wage increases, it led initially to a recession. But in retrospect, the strategy worked and laid the groundwork for a higher-skill, higher-cost economy that we have today.

Today we are undergoing another restructuring. In all likelihood this will not be the last such restructuring. Singapore's version of creative destruction will have to undergo periodic, perhaps 20 year cycles of forced restructuring. But whilst this will inevitably be disruptive, it is fundamentally necessary, and government needs to stay the course despite industry lobbying.

What does deserve worry, however, is worsening income inequality. There are no magic bullets, only a multitude of measures, of which I will propose two.

One reason for Singapore's high income inequality is the high wage differential between different job vocations. Among all the OECD economies, Singapore has the highest income differential between a doctor or lawyer on one hand, and a construction worker or retail assistant, on the other. Our gap in fact is double that in Western European countries, and even much higher than that in Hong Kong.

For example, where the wage gap between a doctor and construction worker may be four or five times in Europe, ours is about 10 times.

There are two reasons for this. First, a large workforce of low-cost, low-skill foreign workers depresses the wages of everyone in that wage band, regardless of nationality. Second, our educational system creates a large differential in starting salaries between the technical versus university graduates.

There are two possible ways to address these two causes of our problems.

First, we can perhaps devise a more innovative immigration program where foreign workers are seen less as a necessary evil but more as one element, and a positive one, in an overall population strategy which does not distinguish so much between foreigner and Singaporean, but recognises their mutual dependency. Instead of just drastically curtailing their influx, the focus could be on finding ways to drastically increase their wages, skills and productivity. And very importantly, to provide economic incentives to create desired outcomes.

Current immigration policy with its punitive foreign worker levy may

Current immigration policy with its punitive foreign worker levy may be simply counter-productive.

be simply counter-productive. It raises the cost of employing them but does not reduce the demand, and furthermore attracts lower-skilled workers because the better ones prefer to go to countries where the take home pay is higher.

> **The two-year "use and discard" approach to foreign workers, besides being socially less than humane, is also simply bad economics.**

The levy could instead be converted into each worker's deferred savings account — similar to the CPF — to be withdrawn upon his permanent repatriation so as to ensure good behaviour whilst in Singapore. Immediately and without an increase in cost to employers, the quality of foreign workers will go up since the higher-skilled ones will be attracted here. Manipulation of both levers — the immediate wage and the levy — will provide instruments for policy adjustments.

The two-year "use and discard" approach to foreign workers, besides being socially less than humane, is also simply bad economics. It will be far more productive to institute a philosophy of "in-country" skills upgrading for foreign workers, with the reward being a longer work residency and even higher payments into their so-called savings accounts.

The conversion of levies into CPF look-alike for foreign workers is also the most effective way to ensure voluntary repatriation after the long-term residency has expired.

After each round of economic restructuring, the foreign worker community in our midst should correspondingly, be more skilled — perhaps all will even have a minimum high school education and certified skills. When that happens, we can perhaps see foreign workers as a potential talent pool.

We can sieve through this pool to find a small minority who are self-motivated to attain measurably higher skills through training programs and employer certification, and we reward them by longer-stay residency permits of say five, ten, even fifteen years.

Those who further aspire even further upwards to change their careers or become entrepreneurs, such as domestic helpers becoming nurses, or construction foremen becoming self-employed builders — for whom we need, and for whom our young are not willing to become — can perhaps even find a pathway towards permanent residency and for some, eventual citizenship.

People talk of New York City as an example of how unskilled, uneducated and impoverished immigrants have helped build the most innovative, entrepreneurial city in the world.

But we only need to look back at our own illiterate forefathers who built this nation, to perhaps recognise that not only the rich Chinese tycoon who is able to buy his citizenship, or the super-skilled scientist or investment banker, has the potential to become a citizen.

I am not going to be so romantic as to think that of the 300,000 construction workers we have in our midst that even 10% would even aspire to become citizens. But I think building that pathway is not only important for the people that may move along that pathway, it sends a more important message to others who would not choose that pathway.

Second, perhaps education pathways can be re-designed to help reduce income inequality. Although much admired for its rigour, Singapore's rigid, linear pathways reflect the university bias of the Anglo-Saxon model. The Institutes of Technical Education (ITEs) generally absorb those who do not do well in normal secondary schools. Although changing slightly, the Polytechnics still mainly absorb those who do not qualify to enter the university preparatory schools, appropriately called Junior Colleges. University is the apex of a single pathway to educational success.

This is reflected by statistics. The starting salary of a Singapore university graduate is about 30%–35% higher than a Poly graduate, whilst in Europe the gap is only about 10%–15%. The gap is much higher for an ITE graduate.

This narrower differential in Europe is achieved by purposefully ensuring that a technical education is genuinely almost as good as a university degree. Switzerland and Germany practice what they call a dual education system where high school graduates can choose either option. Both the technical education and university tracks are equally rigorous in their different ways and technical education in these countries is an attractive option, not a fallback for failing to enter university.

There are possibly two things we can do to reduce the income gap between technical and university graduates.

First, we can amend the technical school — meaning Polytechnic — educational pathway so that their students graduate at the same age as university graduates, and have starting salaries closer to graduates.

This can be done with a longer industry attachment and genuine apprenticeship programs which provide much deeper (and equitably paid) work experience and job knowledge. Industry involvement in apprenticeship and curriculum development is far higher in Europe than here.

Second, we can increase the intersecting pathways by which early entrants into vocational training can cross back into Polytechnic or university streams. Today, the rarity of an ITE graduate making it to university justifies a news headline; this should become normal in future.

Our vocational and technical schools are recognised as best of class around the world. But our graduates do not receive sufficient status, which is reflected in their salaries.

Vocational guilds in Europe generate artisanal pride in and status for their members, by providing professional certification and self-regulation. In Singapore, however, this legally recognised authority is only reserved for the traditionally very elite professions such as law and medicine.

Ironically, such powers are not sought after by industry associations because their members are companies which will only lose out if their employees can be able, with professional certification, to practice on their own, like lawyers and doctors. Government needs to take the lead here.

Finally, I would like to make two "soft" suggestions which would not normally be associated with "hard" economics.

But just as we talk about corporate, social or political culture, there is also an economic culture which shapes how people behave in an economy.

My first suggestion is that Singapore can take the lead in defining new and more holistic indices for economic progress,

Singapore can take the lead in defining new and more holistic indices for economic progress, which take into account factors such as human well-being, environmental sustainability, and socio-cultural development.

which take into account factors such as human well-being, environmental sustainability, and socio-cultural development. Bhutan's gross national happiness index is too touchy-feely on one extreme, but traditional indices like GDP and GNP are on the other extreme, generally accepted as too crude, and worse, promote a lopsided, unsustainable depletion of resources and destruction of the environment. The Australian Bureau of Statistics has actually launched a decade ago, an ambitious program to conduct a Measure of Australia's Progress (MAP), which is tailored to Australia's own unique context.

There are two self-interested reasons for this suggestion.

First, Singapore has already established a reputation as a sustainable city of the future, and getting international acceptance for a measurable yardstick of holistic development can only increase our soft power and brand positioning globally.

Second and perhaps more important, there is a need to counter the complacency of affluence with a compelling vision for our young to aspire towards, measured by more than per capita GDP growth or billionaires per square mile. In other words, even if others don't want to measure against us, we should measure ourselves against our own yardsticks of holistic progress.

My final suggestion is that inclusion, diversity and freedom of expression needs to be pro-actively cultivated if we want to attract the best global talent for innovation in knowledge-based, creative industries, from artificial intelligence to bio-mechanics.

An interesting study once showed a close correlation between those US cities with an actively pro-gay culture, and the number of high-tech start-ups and creative enterprises. The study tentatively concluded that gays tend to be disproportionately represented in these industries. Upon further research however, it found that conclusion to be untrue, Apple's CEO Tim Cook notwithstanding. The number of gays in any industry is largely the same. Instead, the researchers found that many totally straight, decidedly geeky or nerdy people, from scientists to artists to writers, often interpreted a pro-gay culture simply as a bellwether for tolerance.

And most innovative people are generally very individualistic and even eccentric, and like to live in environments where diversity rather than conformity is the daily ethos.

Further studies found the same correlation between the number of publications, theatres, and art galleries in a city, with the presence of innovative companies. These were signals or symbols of a society which promotes the freedom of expression.

The point here is that whilst tourists may come to Singapore for our mega-attractions, whether car races, casinos, or massive plant conservatories, the people we really want — indeed, need — to attract to Singapore to spearhead entrepreneurial innovation, come for different reasons. Our clean, safe, physical environment is of course important. But beyond that, a culture of freedom, inclusion and diversity is very important — perhaps even more than tax incentives.

I shall close here with the recollection that I chose to study economics in university not because it was the closest to a respectable science, which I was always bad at, but because I believe at its very core, economics is about human behaviour, human foibles and human aspirations, and how these collide and collude to enable human society to make mistakes and yet ultimately to progress.

On the eve of yet another exciting chapter of our history, I am confident that our people can come together to ensure that our economy will not only make us materially better off, but it can, with the proper policies, enable the cohesive diversity which I have always held as a vision, to truly become a reality.

Questions and Answers
Moderator: Lee Tzu Yang

Question: You mentioned a digital revolution. How should Singapore cope with this in the next 50 years?

Ho Kwon Ping (HKP): I don't know exactly. But from what I've read, the digital revolution will have the effect of essentially disrupting a lot, and destroying a lot of jobs in standardised routinised areas, which even require cognitive ability. My only suggestion is that it behooves all of us who are engaged in business, in whatever business we are in, to recognise — that's why I used the analogy of the tsunami — that it's coming our way and to understand what that specific tsunami impact may mean for our own business and to take action regarding that. We may find that certain sectors are not going to be affected and certain sectors are going to be decimated. I know that there is actually quite a lot of work going on, including lots of conferences about this topic, which goes into it in a more specific and detailed manner, which I can't do here.

Question: Do you foresee us being a part of Malaysia again in the next 50 years?

HKP: From a theoretical economic perspective, the logic for a Malaysia and Singapore being one is utterly compelling. The People's Action Party (PAP) leadership lobbied very hard for merger back then. But today, the direction that Singapore has moved towards, the values that we have developed as totally core to us and what Malaysia has moved towards are so fundamentally different that I cannot possibly see a union happening in 50 years. A question to ask, which is more germane, that ties in with the issue of security is: Will relations with Malaysia possibly improve more in the next 50 years or will it remain the same, or will it worsen?

That's an important subject. But as to whether Singapore and Malaysia could become one again politically, I cannot, for the life of me, paint a scenario there as to why any Singaporean would ever do it, and, therefore, the only way we would ever be reunited with Malaysia in my view is if it's by physical coercion, which means they come here or we go there.

Question: You touched a bit on price control in terms of housing, which is a very fraught subject. I think you're suggesting that we actually create a more managed system, which allows public housing to move into the private housing developers' hands? But a central concern is that home values have outstripped income growth of the owners.

HKP: No. The discussion is not whether housing prices should be set by the market or not — HDB prices are already set by the government, there is only free market for resale homes. My point is that you have one single developer of housing, which is the HDB. This could change to a situation where HDB still determines prices, but allows different developers to come in. You'd have a lot more differential quality in the market. But these developers can only price homes at whatever the HDB decides. So there would be no issue of inequity. The only thing you would have, of course, is that income which would have gone to government, now goes to the developer. But then could you argue that this would result in a more robust property development market? In Singapore, unlike in other countries like America or elsewhere, you only have very big developers and no smaller developers.

The HDB giving up its role as developer but adding to its role as price regulator doesn't philosophically affect the primary role of government, which is to ensure housing remains affordable. But you would have better quality, differential quality and more competition. The social argument for this is that you can also break down the social divide of 80% of our people living in public housing built mostly by the HDB and 20% living in private housing built by developers.

Question: You suggested having an indicator of how well Singapore is doing beyond its GDP and GNP. Should this be a composite of existing measurements, or should we be measuring something else that could become more important in the next 50 years?

HKP: We are masters of measurement — I don't think there's anything in Singapore that is not measured. Australia has the Measures of Australia's Progress (MAP), which is a holistic measure of national progress beyond the GDP. Given their own unique circumstances, it's the weightage they give on various indices that they take to be a measure of the country's progress. We can take inspiration from that. It is not unrealistic for us in Singapore to look at our own indices and to create one single index which we — after having a national conversation — decide to use as our own index of well-being.

The debate on what a single index should be will also provide us with a forum to discuss the key issues facing Singapore. We would be able to understand a little bit more about what drives us as a society.

Question: The common notion is that too much government in business stifles entrepreneurship. Can you comment on that?

HKP: I've never believed that. There are concerns about a crowding out effect by government companies that are run so well and so effectively that they move into other areas that SMEs can go into. I think that the government is quite aware of that danger. But we all have to be realistic. If you look at Singapore's economic history, we were not like Hong Kong which had the bases of shipping and manufacturing businesses business, and in 1949 a lot of Shanghai industrialists moved there.

Singapore, after independence, had a deficit of local entrepreneurs and local capital. When the government-linked companies were set up, they filled an absolutely necessary role. They have been critical for our growth. The question here is, should the government totally divest itself of certain businesses? You're beginning to see some of that already and maybe they will divest themselves of other companies that are not considered core. But to me, I don't see that as a 50-year question because I don't see it as a fundamental issue. I think the relationship between the private sector and government linked companies is not an unhealthy one. I think government is doing its best to try to nurture SMEs to come up. And MNCs are still going to be required. You cannot forget the smallness of the Singapore economy.

I also don't want to over-romanticise entrepreneurship and think that if you don't have the Singapore Airlines, and the Neptune Orient Lines (NOL), and the Singapore Technologies of the world, we, great entrepreneurs are going to come in there and be able to generate all the employment to keep all our school leavers employed. I think that is romanticising entrepreneurship. I think we entrepreneurs, we need SMEs, and we definitely need government-linked companies to have the guts and the willingness to suffer losses, to probably go into new areas that your Singapore entrepreneurs will not go into.

Question: Is there a possibility that the government would re-assess the MNC model of tax breaks and institute certain policies to encourage more hiring of Singaporeans?

HKP: If we want more Singaporeans to go up the corporate ladder, to the C-suite and so on, clearly, one of the ways to encourage that is to encourage the growth of more Singapore companies. We should absolutely do that. But it should not be at the expense of trying to reduce the number of multinationals or to constrain the performance of multinationals in Singapore. It's almost analogous to the idea that if you have income inequality in a country, should you just tax the rich and level down, or should you let people level up? My solution for the lack of CEOs in companies in Singapore is to level up, have more Singapore companies. That would be the broad philosophical approach. That does not necessarily mean, by the way, that Singapore companies necessarily will hire more Singaporeans.

I think we should also look at another factor and that is, how employable are our own people? I've been on the board of quite a number of global MNCs. In one of the largest companies, the CEO is an Indian national and the whole company has got a lot of Indians. Why Indians? Because they are generally more willing to move around the world. Highly-trained capable Indians don't have a lot of job opportunities in India.

If we want our Singaporeans to really go into the C-suites of multinationals, we have to look at Singaporeans who are willing to move every three to five years to different places. If you work for Unilever, you better be sure that at the age of 25, you join Unilever if you want to be the CEO at 55, you would have moved to probably 15 locations for Unilever. Are our people willing to do that? I see that problem within my own company. I want my general managers to be Singaporeans. The Singaporeans all tell me "I want to go to Shanghai, I want to go to New York, but I don't want to go here or here."

So while we need to promote Singapore firms and Singaporean workers, it's not by reducing multinationals coming here. I do not think that if a Singaporean really wants to rise to the top of an American MNC, he or she is going to be denied that opportunity because of their nationality. We should be a little bit less nationalistic, and not say we got a glass ceiling. But if you're a woman, I would say definitely you got a problem. I do believe there's a glass ceiling for women in a lot of companies. But if you're a Singaporean male, it doesn't matter what ethnic background you are, I think your chances are pretty fair from what I see in C suites around the world.

LECTURE III

SECURITY AND SUSTAINABILITY

Good evening and welcome to the half-way point of this marathon lecture series. I did not fully realise the enormity of my undertaking when I decided to talk about Singapore in the next 50 years, with almost no narrowing of focus to specific subjects. By the time this series is over I shall be an amateur instant expert on everything in the world, which I guess is like the typical Singapore voter.

The first lecture dealt with politics in Singapore in the next 50 years; the second focussed on our economic landscape. This third lecture is titled "Security and Sustainability."

Now, I should explain my interpretation of the word "sustainability" for tonight's lecture. I am explicitly not defining "sustainability" in its environmental context. Whilst this is an important subject on which Singapore has much to contribute, to the extent that there are already two academic institutes dedicated to this subject, I will leave it to them or to the next S R Nathan Fellow to explore this broad area.

Even this attempt to narrow the scope of discussion leaves a frustratingly diverse landscape to cover. Therefore, to impose a conceptual framework, I am categorising security and sustainability into four dimensions: external, internal, civil, and societal. I further focus, perhaps arbitrarily, on some specific policy issues which I believe can enhance the sustainability of existing measures in each security dimension.

Sustainability is not defined just in practical terms of say, resource constraints and capabilities, but also in terms of keeping pace with the changing values of an evolving society, particularly with our younger generation wanting more voice and participation in policy creation.

Using this framework, let me propose and discuss specific policies in each security dimension.

First, External Security

My assumption — to me a self-evident truth actually — is that the strategic vulnerability of Singapore will always dictate the need for a strong military deterrence. Therefore, I've assumed there is no need to even discuss this point: after all, an IPS survey has shown that an overwhelming 98% of Singaporeans support national service.

Unfortunately, the survey also revealed that the main reason for supporting National Service (NS) is that it is "good for our boys". The actual military rationale is not apparently the key consideration.

This would be a serious case of misplaced enthusiasm. Despite its success as a nation-building tool, deterrence must always be the primary reason for national service. The prolonged peace and stability we enjoy today, which many take for granted and as evidence that a strong deterrence is no longer necessary, is precisely and ironically because of that very same deterrence.

The difficulty of course, for Government to convince Singaporeans about potential threats, is that speaking about them only creates unnecessary tension with our neighbours and gives fodder for potential enemies to criticise us for scare-mongering.

I am under the same self-imposed censorship here: public settings are not appropriate venues to discuss the nature of our security threats nor raise convincing examples of the reality of that threat.

Therefore, I am reduced at this forum to simply remind ourselves that the politics of pragmatism or realpolitik, rather than wishful thinking, must always underpin Singapore's foreign policy; and so we must realise that geography is destiny. We are destined to be, with our immediate neighbours, sometimes the best of friends, and sometimes much less so.

What Theodore Roosevelt said about speaking softly but carrying a big stick, and what Lee Kuan Yew said about Singapore being only a small shrimp in the ocean, but a poisonous one — these should probably be the pithy quotes inscribed on Singapore Armed Forces Training Institute (SAFTI)'s walls for all young Singapore Armed Forces (SAF) officers to read. A strong SAF is a strategic imperative, given our geo-political history and position.

And, therefore, we need to find ways to maintain, against the spectre of an ageing and declining population, the deterrent capability of not just our regular, but particularly our reserve forces. Even with outsourcing of some NS jobs and restructuring of organisational structures, a critical mass of reserve soldiers remains important even in an age of advanced technology and weaponry.

This starting point brings me to the proverbial elephant in the room that I will always identify at each lecture. But this time it is a she-elephant.

The question here is simple: will the time ever come when universal female conscription becomes necessary? And even if it does not become an absolute necessity, should we prepare for the possible eventuality, given the very long time-frame required for debate and preparation before any implementation?

After all, much debate and preparation will clearly be necessary. There is a huge caveat or qualifier to the overwhelming 98% support of NS by our citizens. The same IPS survey revealed that only 9% of all Singaporean women surveyed — and 13% of those under 30 — supported female conscription. A different study found broadly the same results: a higher proportion — 22% — of Singaporean women support female conscription, but only 9% said they were willing to do it for two years. In other words, it's great for my father, husband, boyfriend, or son to do NS, but not me.

If we are to change the views of young Singaporean women about female conscription — which by the way is gender-neutral in the Conscription Act — the first challenge is to convince them that there is indeed a demographic dilemma. Going by past attempts to raise the issue and the lukewarm response, I think a lot of convincing remains to be done.

Current demographic trends from the United Nations, shows that in a "no-change" scenario — meaning we assume current Total Fertility Rates (TFR) and no in-migration — the male population aged 15 to 24 will decline by around 35% between 2015 and 2040: a drop of one-third in 25 years. The rate of decline will continue so that in 50 years time — by 2065 — the same male NS-age cohort then will be less than half of its size today.

While acknowledging this trend, Ministry of Defence (MINDEF) has also said that with technological advances and organisational restructuring, the SAF can retain its same deterrent ability. Of course, I have no reasons to doubt MINDEF. However, the flip side of this point is that, by the same token, these same technologies requiring more brain than brawn, are inherently female-friendly and will increasingly enable women to serve meaningful roles in the military.

As the nature of warfare changes, the classic image of thousands of foot-soldiers charging up a hill will necessarily evolve, possibly to one with armed drones skilfully and remotely controlled — by women.

Today, women make up 33% of the Israeli Defense Forces, 15% of the US military, and 7 % of the SAF regular forces. More than 90% of the positions in the IDF are available for female soldiers. Starting next year in 2016, 100% of vocations in the US military will be eligible for women.

While it is premature today to conclude that military conscription for two years for women will definitely become necessary, I would argue that we need to start changing mindsets soon. Otherwise it will be too late should the need actually arise one day.

One way is to introduce universal female conscription for a form of non-military, shorter-term duration focussed on supporting our civil defence, Home Team, and even community and healthcare institutions. This is not dissimilar to efforts already in place such as our Volunteer Youth Corps scheme, which should, however, augment and not replace the need

One way is to introduce universal female conscription for a form of non-military, shorter-term duration focussed on supporting our civil defence, Home Team, and even community and healthcare institutions.

to conscript females to meet our demographic challenge. After all, to bolster these capabilities is part of the notion of Total Defence which encompasses more than just the military.

Universal female conscription serves two purposes. One, it is socially unhealthy for our female citizens to support national service for men but to believe that serving the nation, even in non-military ways, is not required of them. A national service ethos and pride should be inculcated in our young women in the next 50 years of nation-building.

Two, should it ever become necessary to conscript women into military service, the challenge will then be only logistical and technical, and at least not attitudinal.

Universal female conscription could start with the Ministry of Culture, Community and Youth (MCCY), Ministry of Education (MOE) and our Singapore Civil Defence Force (SCDF) taking the lead, and with MINDEF only providing whatever necessary technical support, so that this massive undertaking does not divert our military from its main role.

It could last several months and be held during the interlude between graduating from secondary school and entering tertiary institutions or entering the work force. Decentralised to the schools level for logistical purposes but with expertise provided by the uniformed services — the Home Team as well as SAF — the program organised by MCCY could comprise a mix of school-level day classes, field practices, and Outward Bound style residential training. An annual equivalent of reservist training lasting several weeks during school term breaks could enhance the re-learning and refinement of para-medical, para-civil defence, or para-police capabilities.

The intention is to train future generations of female citizens who are not just actively engaged in the ongoing Total Defence of the nation, but also equipped with real life skills which are different from, but no less important than, their male counterparts. Singapore in the next 50 years will certainly need a far more comprehensive voluntary services sector; national service-women could clearly contribute to their country in this area.

An important point, however, is that to maintain the fundamental ethos of universal national service, it should be truly universal for all Singaporean young women and not just be on a volunteer basis.

An interesting but slightly different parallel can be found in the Nordic countries, which are small and affluent like Singapore, currently enjoying peace but never complacent about external threats. Their approach is to embed universal conscription into law and have it become a socially acceptable norm, but without necessarily rolling it out full-scale unless the need arises.

In Norway, for example, national service for one year for women has just become law. However, their system of conscription is universal liability for the sake of equality but actual call up is far less than the liable pool. Less than 10% of liable men and women are actually called up, and recruitment is based on self-motivation plus physical and mental fitness. But to maintain psychological readiness, universal conscription is embedded into law. Denmark has a similar system, and Sweden will soon introduce the same.

Let me now move from external to the three dimensions of domestic security which I define as internal security, civil security, and societal security, to reflect their very different orientations.

Internal Security

I define internal security threats as clandestine and potentially violent activities which seek to subvert and undermine the ideological foundations of the state. These would be threats which mainly but not necessarily, culminate in terrorist activities. There are different origins of such threats — communism 50 years ago and Islamic radicalism today. To mainly deal with the communist threat, the British colonial government introduced, and it continues as law today, the Internal Security Act (ISA), which has as its main feature, the right of indefinite preventive detention without being charged nor tried in court.

Once a very controversial issue and heavily criticised by Western governments and NGO's, preventive detention has become grudgingly accepted as a necessary and hopefully limited violation of civil liberties, as these same governments try to combat terrorism in their own societies.

Post 9/11, the United States government, in particular, has embraced indefinite preventive detention. Recent terrorist events in Europe by their own citizens have even raised questions as to whether preventive detention should have been used more aggressively.

The point is that potential abuse resides in any government with unconstrained powers, regardless of political heritage or ideology.

The debate, therefore, has shifted in recent years from calls for outright abolition of the ISA and its equivalents, into the need to ensure that this unconstrained, extraordinary power does not become abused.

Lest anyone think that concern about potential abuse of the ISA implies, automatically, a distrust of the current government and the PAP, we should remember that in a 50-year time horizon, it might well be a newly-elected, non-PAP government which might give cause for worry. The point is that potential abuse resides in any government with unconstrained powers, regardless of political heritage or ideology.

Proponents for the abolition of the ISA argue that preventive detention can still be preserved under other legislation, such as an anti-terrorism act. My own sense is that if one accepts the principle of preventive detention, then whether we keep the ISA or replace it by a similar act, makes not much difference. My primary concern is that preventive detention must not be unconstrained and must have checks and balances which serve the legitimate purposes of security agencies whilst making abuse more difficult, if not entirely impossible.

For example, the right to detain a person for an initial one year period — possibly reduced from the current two year — should remain unconditional and unconstrained.

However, subsequent detention periods could require a higher degree of external review than currently provided for — say, two high court justices rather than the current single judge and two persons appointed by the President. Failure to achieve unanimous approval for further detention would trigger a process of further review by for example, a non-partisan panel comprising members of the legislature. There could also be a cap on the maximum number of consecutive detention periods unless specifically approved by a similar legislative panel.

Such measures cannot fully prevent abuse by an all-powerful government, but in a parliamentary system with at least some opposition representation, true national-security threats as opposed to opponents or critics of a ruling party, can be differentiated and abuses brought to public attention.

A society which allows preventive detention should be acutely aware of the risks this brings to its own hard-won, much-cherished freedoms and civil liberties. Such a society must reflect deeply on the need for a balance between a government requiring extraordinary powers to deal with extraordinary threats, and a civil society requiring space to freely express its views without fear of detention.

In the next 50 years, the search for this balance will be dynamic and changing as the threats to internal security will change. What must not change is the constant awareness that any people who surrender too much extraordinary powers to any government, does so at its own peril.

Civil Security

Let me now move to civil security, which deals with the relationship between the individual and the state on issues related to crime and punishment. My question here relates to the sustainability of various forms of punishment into the next 50 years as we become an increasingly affluent, mature, and presumably more compassionate, "civilised" and humane society. Can we modify and eventually abolish some possibly "cruel and unusual" punishments without sacrificing our notably, and laudably, low levels of crime?

What is appropriate punishment in one era may not be so in another period; indeed, the assumption behind the concept of "cruel and unusual punishment" in American jurisprudence is the notion that what constitutes cruelty and unusualness, so to speak, depends on current social norms. The practice of branding convicts on the cheek by hot irons was the

> **To the extent that the duality of crime versus punishment reflects the values of a society, our 50th anniversary is a good time to reflect on how our evolving values will affect our criminal code.**

norm in 17th century America or Europe but by the 19th century it would be considered cruel and unusual. The same for flogging and whipping.

To the extent that the duality of crime versus punishment reflects the values of a society, our 50th anniversary is a good time to reflect on how our evolving values will affect our criminal code.

I refer specifically to the practice of caning, which might have been the norm in the past century, but which would certainly be construed as cruel and unusual punishment in the First World, to which we apparently have arrived and want to remain in, at least in terms of wealth.

There are two different approaches in the arguments against caning.

First is the notion that it is by itself barbaric and should be abolished.

Second is the notion that even if one were to reluctantly consider this a necessary punishment for some offences, it should in some vaguely moral way be appropriate to the crime — that a physically injurious punishment should be restricted only to physically injurious offences.

This concession to retaining caning for violent crimes such as rape or grievous hurt has no basis in legal philosophy; but at least it meets the human desire for some kind of moral retribution, not unlike the Biblical injunction of an eye for an eye, a life for a life.

But even this concession would find unacceptable the practice of caning for offences such as spraying graffiti on public walls, or for money lending by loan sharks, or for overstaying a visa. All these offences and more, now provide for caning.

What started out in colonial times as caning for hardened criminals and violent triad gangsters — who incidentally were not Europeans and, therefore, not worthy of the same humanity — is now meted out for a very wide range of offences with little relationship to each other, except perhaps that they were social problems at the time and caning was seen to be the most effective deterrent.

Proponents of caning are not shy about the reason for its deterrent impact. It is intentionally brutal and painful. In a rare and candid account with *The Straits Times*, the Director of Prisons once gave a graphic account, parts of which I quote now:

> "The prisoner, stripped of all his clothes, is strapped to a trestle by his ankles and wrists.... Correct positioning is critically important.

If he (the person applying the caning) is too near the prisoner, the tip of the cane will fall beyond the buttocks and ... thus reduce the effect of the stroke.

If he is too far, the stroke will only cover part of the buttocks. Most of the prisoners put up a violent struggle after each of the first three strokes. After that, their struggles lessen as they become weaker. At the end of the caning, those who receive more than three strokes will be in a state of shock. .... Many will collapse, but the medical officer and his team of assistants are on hand to revive them and apply antiseptic on the caning wound. Many will pretend to faint but they cannot fool the prison medical officer whose presence is legally required."

Interestingly, the colonial authorities practised flogging by what is affectionately called a cat-o-nine-tails until 1954, when it was banned. Possibly caning might have been banned a few years later, but in 1959 the PAP took over the government and, indicative of the pragmatism for which it is highly vaunted, decided that what works, should simply remain. And so it has remained for 50 years, and as we moved from Third World to First World, and other countries banned vestiges of centuries past, we added more non-violent offences for which caning was the punishment.

Since we have placed deterrence as the sole reason for a punishment and have abandoned proportionality altogether, one wonders what offences we would not apply the cane to, if the offence became widespread enough. How about e-commerce crimes, which as the papers recently noted, has increased over 200% in the past few years?

As I mentioned earlier, graffiti-spraying, moneylending, repeated drink driving, visa overstaying, were all added after independence. No new offences have been added in recent years, but neither were any removed.

The other egregious use of caning is for young people — something which might surprise most parents here. The minimum age for criminal responsibility is — guess — seven years old. Juvenile offenders between seven and 16 can be caned and put into solitary confinement; they can be imprisoned for life if under 18 years old and be tried in adult courts. Yet you can only vote at 21 years old; is the discrepancy between age of criminal liability and political maturity somewhat unbalanced?

There is clearly no huge public demand for the end of caning or for that matter, for the abolition of capital punishment. To most Singaporeans it is a non-issue. As to whether it is truly a deterrent or not, most people do not really care. If caning helped get us to where we are today as a crime-free society, why abolish it?

Therefore, if our government simply abolished caning, it would not be seen as responding to the desires of the public (since the public is not clamouring for it), and can even be considered irresponsible, if crime rates rise as a result of abolition. But for the sake of a more humane penal system, considering a future without caning is both a governmental as well as social imperative. Thus, a reasonable step a government can do is to impose a moratorium on caning, either selectively, for various crimes, or as a whole, and measure whether the offences increase as a result. There is quite a lot of literature in criminology, about how the actual severity of the sentence is not the main deterrent; it is the speed by which the offender is caught, and the consistency by which punishment is speedily applied, which is the major deterrent against crime.

For example, some believe that caning for graffiti-spraying was introduced in the 1960's because the *Barisan Sosialis* supporters painted politically incendiary slogans on walls and caning was introduced to stop them.

Whether that was justified or not, is for history to decide. But the likelihood of such forms of civil disorder recurring, with tonnes of people spraying graffiti on the walls of Singapore, is not high.

Whether repeated drink driving will increase if offenders are not caned, I do not know, but we can easily find out and measure the consequences. The result should then determine steps after that.

Over time and with the excellent law enforcement we have, I would hope that we can evolve into a relatively crime-free society without the need

At this milestone of our national journey, we should have the moral audacity to question the sustainability of old ideas and aspire for a higher level of human development.

for punishments which belong more to centuries past and not centuries future. But if I am wrong, we can always end the moratorium.

The hallmark of a society progressively evolving towards higher standards of civilised behaviour is its ability and willingness to explore, debate and try out new ideas and test their efficacy. At this milestone of our national journey, we should have the moral audacity to question the sustainability of old ideas and aspire for a higher level of human development.

A moratorium on capital punishment follows the same logic as for caning. But it would be unrealistic to think that this will happen without first achieving a positive result from a moratorium on caning.

However, we can tighten the criteria for capital punishment so that offences such as causing death but simply intending to cause injury, being just involved in a group which has caused a death, do not incur the death penalty. As for drug trafficking, an end to the mandatory death penalty and giving more leeway to judges, which was recently implemented, is clearly, in my view, a step in the right direction.

The challenge will be to maintain the laudable public safety for which Singapore is famous, while also progressively reducing the physically injurious and ultimately lethal forms of punishment.

Ultimately, in the march of humanity towards civilisation, one consistent marker throughout all these centuries, is how society punishes its offenders and not just how it rewards its heroes.

Societal Security

I now come to societal security. The challenges to Singapore's societal cohesion have always been religious and racial cleavages. The PAP's fundamental approach to this security issue has been to vigorously promote a multicultural and multiracial society with very robustly

Ultimately, in the march of humanity towards civilisation, one consistent marker throughout all these centuries, is how society punishes its offenders and not just how it rewards its heroes.

articulated and consistently protected rights for every minority to practise its traditions.

No tolerance is allowed for any community, whether racial or religious, to infringe on, dominate or insult another. Instead of assimilation, where minorities are encouraged to jump into a melting pot and emerge as the same people, Singapore has always espoused integration, whereby people retain their racial and religious traditions, but respect the rights of the other.

These policies have been widely lauded by all observers, and is no small achievement when contrasted against serious racial or religious cleavages in developed countries such as the USA, or for that matter, in France as we have recently seen. Singapore's commitment to racial and religious harmony and equality of opportunity for all communities, was never just an aspiration, vision or ideal, but an imperative for survival.

But even with this extremely laudable tradition, we can still do more to enhance social cohesion, especially at this juncture of history when new challenges also present new opportunities.

The opportunity is to gradually and carefully open up debate on the most sensitive racial and religious issues so that we achieve the full transparency, candour and mutual trust between racial and religious groups which marks a truly mature society, without the divisive tragedies of societies which allow totally free expression even at the risk of inflaming already volatile and emotional issues.

Singapore if it has erred at all, has been on the side of caution, so that the slightest discussion of anything potentially divisive in the realm of race and religion, is considered out of bounds. European nations have erred, on the other hand, in allowing such freedom of expression as resulted in the tragic Charlie Hebdo massacres.

I believe that erring on the side of caution is the right approach, but in the next 50 years we can gradually introduce more transparency and candour in the discussion of race and religion so that our societal security can flourish with fewer and fewer OB markers.

For example, ethnic quotas in HDB estates and mandatory ethnic representation in electoral constituencies are publicly known policies, but statistics and policies on the ethnic composition of the national service army and police are considered too sensitive for open discussion. Demographic data on new migrants are not openly available, but birth rates of different races in Singapore are public information. There seems to be not a high amount of consistency on what is deemed sensitive or not, and what is confidential versus publicly available information.

It can be argued that the traditional fault lines of CMIO — Chinese, Malay, Indian, and Other — are transforming as new fault lines emerge.

The so called curry wars where Singaporeans of all races lined up against new citizens from China who objected to curry aromas from their neighbours in their HDB estate, illustrate that culture and race are intertwined rather than inexorably fixed along simplistic racial lines. The same may be true for Singaporean Malays versus Malays from neighbouring Indonesia and Malaysia. Policies based on presumptions of old fault lines may have to be revisited as we evolve.

Issues of identity shall be the focus of my final lecture, but my point here is simply that societal security requires us to eventually discuss openly the most sensitive issues of race and religion, even at the risk of causing controversy overseas, or bordering into communal politics at home. Sensitive issues are gradually desensitised when they are brought into the open and discussed responsibly and diligently, by all members of that society.

Another area of potential social divisiveness is our new male citizens. The likelihood of their increasing in numbers can only increase, not decrease, because in-migration has to bridge some of the gap between our declining TFR and a consistent if not growing, population. Yet, there are signs of resentment by our NS-men against new citizens who benefit from Singaporean nationality, but need make no sacrifices to obtain their passports.

Adding salt to the wound is the fact that many employers prefer to hire new citizens because they have no reservist liability. Measures to reward reservists do not really solve the problem because many NS-men see them as devices to buy off their disaffection. Neither are reservists asking that new male citizens past NS liability age, serve the full two years which they are required to do. Most seem to simply want concrete demonstration of a willingness by new male citizens to sacrifice some of their time for their new homeland, and to see a genuine desire to be more integrated into the lives of their new compatriots. Inflow of foreign talent is generally regarded positively by Singaporeans, but the issue is not just tolerance. It is about the integration of new citizens into Singapore culture.

This can perhaps be achieved by requiring all new male citizens of reservist liability age to undergo a three-month program which need not comprise residential training but would impart civil defence, para-medical and para-police training, and include an annual reservist liability of a week or two for several years.

This would clearly not be favoured by those new citizens who only want the convenience of a Singapore passport and are willing to invest millions of dollars for it; it may in fact lead to a halt in such applications (which in my mind, is no bad thing).

But for those who genuinely want Singapore to be their home, the opportunity to integrate more into our society and be able to also say with pride they too, serve the country and sacrifice for it, such a program may even be welcomed, provided that the disruption to their lives is not enormous.

In conclusion, Singapore can proudly celebrate its 50 years as a sovereign nation, with some of the best international standards for all its uniformed forces, for its public safety record, and its rigorous adherence to multicultural, multiracial tolerance and mutual respect.

Security in all its dimensions, is a blessing which has taken decades to create and can all too quickly crumble through neglect, carelessness, reckless disregard, or irresponsible changes.

Therefore, we should be cautious about needless tinkering. At the same time, a willingness to change with the times, or indeed to ride on the crest of the tidal waves of history, can prevent the intellectual rigidity which weakens the sustainability of our society as a dynamic and evolving culture.

Unlike general political and economic issues which are subject to shorter time frames based on election and business cycles, fundamental issues concerning society and what values we stand for take longer

By starting this public conversation now, we can build the capacity for discourse and reasoning which should benefit those Singaporeans who will inherit this nation.

to unfold and resolve as they require citizens and civil society to engage in discourse between themselves and with governing institutions. By starting this public conversation now, we can build the capacity for discourse and reasoning which should benefit those Singaporeans who will inherit this nation.

In this, the midpoint of my five-part lecture series, I hope I have started to encourage younger Singaporeans to ponder the big issues of their future and to consider concrete responses. Only after much thinking, then debate and deliberation, can vague ideas become reality.

My next lecture will be on "Demography and Family". Instead of crime and punishment I shall talk about Central Provident Fund (CPF), marriages and babies.

Questions and Answers
Moderator: Ambassador Ong Keng Yong

Question: When you spoke about female conscription, I was also thinking about the men. Do men need to be in a combat role? Or can they also opt for medical or other vocations in the military service, like women?

Ho Kwon Ping (HKP): First, my sense is that if we were to ever have full two year conscription for women into the military, you will find that there are a lot more combat vocations that should be open to women. The US military, the Israeli army have opened up more vocations for women now. The Israeli army, in particular, has redefined the role of infantry so that women can serve in combat positions in infantry but not necessarily at the front line.

When I was talking about the social services that women could do, that was within the context that women can have shorter term conscription to overcome any attitudinal resistance. Theirs could be a three-month programme — for para-defence, para-police, and para-medical.

Clearly, if you read the literature and talk to military leaders today, one concludes that the thinking behind men and women not being able to serve in the military together is an increasingly outdated one. The Norwegian military, for example, was the first in the world to actually have women serve together with men in submarines, which is the most confined setting you could imagine. So I think my answer to you is yes, if we ever had full-time NS for women, it should not be women just doing social services, and men doing the fighting.

Question: You alluded to racial imbalance in NS being an extremely sensitive issue. At what point in the next 50 years can we speak openly about it? Is the Chinese-Malay-Indian-Other (CMIO) framework self-perpetuating in that it prevents us from talking about these issues?

HKP: I will discuss CMIO and all issues on identity, culture and race in my last lecture. On the issue of racial composition in our armed forces, I think the right time is coming for people to discuss this in private settings, in homes, with different friends from different races. I'm not sure the time is right yet, for us to discuss these issues, in a public setting, with the media, with coverage from foreign media. There is a growing perception that issues such as ethnic composition in the police and the army and so on, are being discussed among young people themselves openly. I would encourage this, and I would hope that at some point in time they can become more public, something that perhaps the Institute of Policy Studies (IPS) may wish to do.

Question: It's common for government leaders to say that Singapore society is not mature enough and people are not ready to discuss certain issues. Hence there is censorship. What's your response?

HKP: We are going to have an increasingly active civil society and there must be much greater access to information. I'm not talking about the declassification of classified documents, but I think you'll find that most governments tend to be overly protective of information and it is not that this is necessarily a policy from the Cabinet or the Prime Minister. Generally, information is power and even civil servants would like to give as little information as possible. I think all of you at IPS and at universities, even if you are trying to get the most mundane statistical studies on aspects of Singapore's development will find that it is very difficult to get information. We cannot have a very active and participatory civil society if getting simple information from state agencies is very difficult. So I would support the call for some kind of freedom of information act whereby state agencies are required to disclose information, which is not purposely classified as secret or classified. Obviously, this still allows room for overzealous civil servants to stamp classified on everything, but I think that is a risk that we would have to accept because we cannot be the ones to decide what is classified or unclassified.

Question: How do you discuss sensitive issues respectfully, politely, and not in the Internet troll sort of way? Could you talk a bit about how you think civil society and civil discourse can evolve in the next few decades, in the next 50 years, so that we can get there? So that we can eventually discuss the sensitive issues, that we cannot today discuss in a healthy manner?

HKP: There is a need to move in that direction. The trouble is if you move in that direction, you will clearly upset some people. The question is — to what extent can you allow some upset and still live within the boundaries of a relatively tension-free society? Or do you allow civic discourse to the point that it goes out of control? I don't have a specific answer. But if one were to promote this gradual increase in civil discourse, generally, you will find that most people would say that if you started in a relatively rarefied environment rather than in a mass environment, it is a healthier and easier way to start.

One possibility would be to actually have active discussion of such issues by institutions, such as IPS, whose responsibility is to involve people in discourse. They can bring people of different races and religions together and in a pure Chatham House rules type of situation with zero reportage by the media. Maybe that is one way to start; by actually throwing out relatively sensitive, relatively volatile issues, discussing it within a small group of people who already are committed to knowing that regardless of the temperatures that may rise within the room, they are there for a specific purpose, of trying to increase the level of discourse within society. Universities and academia is are good venues for this. Media is a very poor venue because the media tends to generally inflame and exaggerate views.

Question: You mentioned that employers have the tendency to prefer males who are non-citizens, males who are of NS age. Now, security is very important to Singapore. In the next 50 years, how can government policies be done such that employers will not place Singapore males at a disadvantage in the workplace?

HKP: I would not want to consider any kind of punitive measures, or legal measures, which force employers to have to engage Singaporeans rather than new citizens who don't have NS liability or foreigners. Once we go into that area, it's a very, very slippery slope down which we then create all kinds of protectionism for our male Singaporeans which is very unhealthy. Many larger and smaller companies do this already but it is necessary to recognise that Singaporean male employees who have to go out for two or three weeks every year to do NS are doing something that's important, and they are not to be disadvantaged against those who don't have NS liability. Sometimes companies need to be reminded of that, otherwise they tend to go for the foreigners or the new citizens. But the only solution to me is one of convincing people, not any kind of mandatory measures that require companies to favour Singaporeans who do NS. It has to be voluntary.

Question: Is it worthwhile thinking about dual-nationality, dual-citizenship for Singaporeans?

HKP: This is an issue we need to seriously consider. The historical and traditional line has been that we cannot afford to have Singaporeans who might have dual nationalities because of loyalties and so on. But to what extent are we possibly losing Singaporeans who want to live in another place for the sake of convenience, or other reasons but who would also like to be Singaporeans. I don't have a fixed view on that, not halfway near my relatively aggressive views on the need for military deterrence.

We also need to have more statistics, to see how many Singaporeans we are "losing", because we are forcing them to make a choice.

Question: I was a bit disappointed in how you so beguilingly, with such reasonableness, spoke about the Internal Security Act (ISA). Your conclusion was that we still need it. My sense is if it had not been a mistake 50 or 30 years ago, it's certainly a big mistake to still have the ISA now.

Because it is so powerful, that any government, would just be too seduced to use it. Why do you think it is still necessary?

HKP: Well, we know that both you (referring to Substation Chairman Chew Kheng Chuan, who asked the question) and I have been victims of the ISA. Hence, I do have emotional views about it. But I also have to consider today: If I was running this country and anticipated some of the threats we see in other societies, could I honestly say to myself, if I were today the Prime Minister of Singapore, I would want to abolish the ISA? I can't honestly say I would want to do that, because I do believe there are threats, which cannot be countered by simply bringing people to trial and charging them. The nature of threats to internal security, to the extent that we see them now in the Western World, and you see that even Western governments and NGOs that used to be crying against preventive detention, recognise that preventive detention is necessary in certain circumstances.

A simple abolition of the ISA, a simple abolition of the right of any government to exercise preventive detention without charging a person, can also lead to more dangers. My biggest concern now is the potential abuse of preventive detention by a government for illegitimate reasons, related to its own survival, as opposed to the survival of society. Now how can you prevent that kind of abuse? In my view, you can tinker with the system so that you do not have such a long period of detention, you can tinker with the system so that the external reviews are more rigorous so that rather than government appointees, other people may need to approve it. I'd propose that ultimately this must also be subjected to legislative review because even if you have a ruling government that can exercise preventive detention like in the United States, you have an administration that is in power and it exercises preventive detention, but by having an opposition in congress, ultimately abuses are brought to light, and there is at least a debate on that. So my whole focus now is on how you can create more — and I'm not saying 100 percent — safeguards so that abuse of preventive detention for political reasons can at least be checked more than in the past.

Question: In talking about unusual and cruel punishment, I'm just curious as to how come you chose to talk about caning as opposed to say, the death penalty. Although not on the same scale as caning, the death penalty too has been expanded and now covers drug trafficking as well. Will we be having the same conversation about the death penalty in the next 50 years as we are having about caning now?

HKP: In my view, the death penalty is a punishment, which is still retained by a lot of countries whereas caning is such an unusual punishment that you will find very few countries except those, which had the regional legacies like Malaysia together with Singapore, or Saudi Arabia that has caning.

I'm going for low hanging fruit so to speak. I think it is easier for a society like Singapore to do a survey of punishments around the world to recognise that the kind of caning that we're doing, which we call caning but is actually flogging, or whipping is perhaps something that we can gradually do away with. Capital punishment is still retained by many developed societies so if I were to advocate an end to capital punishment, I think I would be taking a particular position on it, rather than to try to be a disinterested observer and say that essentially caning is so unusual to developed societies and even most other societies except a few like Saudi Arabia and other Arab countries around the world. That perhaps it does not behoove a society that is claiming to have gone from third world to first in one generation to still retain this practice. The second reason is a very practical one. I think you call for an abolition or moratorium of capital punishment but you keep the caning. I think it's a little bit reversed. You could say that the punishment itself is more severe in terms of capital punishment, but it is a more common punishment.

Question: You were talking about cleavages and new fault lines coming up and I realise that you didn't talk about the increasing income gap. As a student, I feel the income gap is becoming more evident in schools. Do you see this as a big problem? Secondly, my schoolmates and I have to volunteer as part of a Community Involvement Programme (CIP) for students. There is a huge gap between volunteers and beneficiaries — the former see themselves as helping poor people and there is a gap between them. If my schoolmates are going to be policymakers next time, isn't it a big issue if they feel they are making policies for a separate group of people?

HKP: I think those are very serious questions. On the issue of greater income inequality in our academic institutions, I would assume that what you are referring to is the fact that increasingly, it is the children of university graduates who get into the universities and the good Junior Colleges (JCs).

This is an insidious self-perpetuating cycle which you can't block — the children of well-off families tend to do better. It's self-reinforcing. You find that generally the children of doctors become doctors; a lot of children of lawyers become lawyers. I know the government has looked at this issue. But it is a social problem because our schools are highly meritocratic. We do have an insidious system now that is not easy to change. You cannot create barriers for the children of university graduates to go into university. But it is getting harder for the children of non-university educated parents to get into university. All I can say is I know that Ministry of Education (MOE) is very aware of this, but these are social issues that have to be dealt with.

The other issue that possibly can be dealt with more, and I know MOE is trying to deal with it in some ways, is elitism within our own educational establishment. I have long been a critic of these kinds of elitism, which is manifested in the gifted programme, in streaming and in many other ways. Minister Heng Swee Keat has tried to institute a new system whereby there is less grading of schools, but then there is a counter reaction from families. Families whose children do go to top schools get very offended if there is no more ranking because they want their children to belong to the top-ranked schools. This is an area where it is not as sensitive as race and religion is, but it is a critical issue that involves everyone and it is an issue where there should be a lot more debate because it is not that sensitive and yet, it is highly complex. So I hope you'll raise more of these issues when you attend other forums.

Question: Singapore has gone through decades of success and some Singaporeans feel we are entitled to succeed. Hence, some in my generation are feeling disillusioned with their lot in life, they feel they are not succeeding. Then we have people who are increasingly unhappy about the income gap. Will our unhappiness have an effect on national security? Secondly, the same generation of entitled Singaporeans are being outperformed by more driven, more competitive, more hardworking immigrants. How will this affect our sustainability as a country?

HKP: I cannot fault the younger generation for feeling more entitled. They grew up in a far more stable and secure Singapore, a far more affluent Singapore than their parents grew up in. So to only constantly chide them and say "Oh, you know, you are being complacent, you feel entitled, you're not as competitive as these very hungry immigrants from Myanmar or from China", that grates against many of the young Singaporeans I talk to who basically say "Look, we grew up in this society of wealth and affluence and so on, so how can you tell us to be as hungry as the people coming here from China and Myanmar?". I think there's some validity when they say that.

What one can do is to constantly remind one's self that this complacency, this entitlement, is dangerous. It is the responsibility not just of the older leaders but our own young people themselves, to see that this is a danger. Young Singaporeans who travel overseas must be acutely aware of the differences between Singapore and the outside world. They must be acutely aware not to be so paternalistic and judgemental. When Singaporeans travel overseas and see the dirtiness in Jakarta, and the poverty in Vietnam, and they just look at it disdainfully, that is clearly one of the problems we have. This problem can be solved, very easily, if we ever hit a super bad recession, and have massive layoffs among Singaporeans. But it is rather ironic that we would have to go through this in order for Singaporeans not to feel entitled. That's not a solution one would want to have. The only other solution one can think of having is really a combination between older people telling Singaporeans about this problem, but particularly younger Singaporeans talking among themselves because you've a lot more street cred when you talk to each other than when your parents tell you that you're entitled and you're spoilt and you're soft.

LECTURE IV

DEMOGRAPHY AND FAMILY

Good evening and welcome to the fourth IPS-Nathan Lecture, as part of the S R Nathan Fellowship for the Study of Singapore. Tonight's topic is "Demography and Family", which should be a rather tame and sedate topic, dealing with genteel ageing and gentle babies. But as I researched this topic I found that it is in fact a raging cauldron of highly emotional issues because it touches all of us very personally.

I will deal with two issues at opposite ends of the life-cycle spectrum: how to provide for people in retirement, and how to encourage young people to have babies.

To recognise the new year, I shall not call them my proverbial elephants any more, but instead, my bearded ram and baby goat in the room.

The first issue is retirement adequacy. The government's promise to Singaporeans at independence 50 years ago was that every hard-working citizen would be able to own a decent home through the Housing & Development Board (HDB), and to save enough money through the Central Provident Fund (CPF), to fund living expenses throughout retirement. These promises were a critical part of the social compact between citizen and state, and have, largely, been met. However, because of increasing life expectancy, the CPF has been increasingly stressed to provide enough cash for retirement, and changes, some of them controversial, have been made to the original terms of the CPF in the past three decades.

Further measures which tweak the increasingly complex CPF have just been announced, including increasing the contributions from older employees as well as their employers, and raising the salary ceiling.

The CPF advisory panel has also made new proposals, and a new Silver Support Scheme (SSS) has just been launched. These have all clearly helped to strengthen retirement adequacy. There are differing views as to whether they go far enough to actually provide sufficient retirement funding for the lower-income retirees, but such differences of opinion are to be expected.

Instead, I don't wish to dwell on these more immediate issues, but to ask a more long term question. Because of the continuing erosion of the CPF's ability, by itself, to provide retirement adequacy, the scheme is on one hand being continually tweaked and on the other, is being supplemented by external schemes such as the SSS. Further down the road, yet other schemes may be announced.

Instead of the CPF retaining its place as the centrepiece and the cornerstone of the Singapore retirement system, current trends may eventually relegate it to being just one component in an increasingly disparate and complicated collection of retirement-related schemes. The danger is that people will fail to fully understand, much less appreciate, the totality of the many separate schemes now in place and yet to come in the next 50 years, and may be perplexed by the state's role in ensuring retirement adequacy. Should that happen, a creeping cynicism may start to undermine the social contract which the CPF in its simple boldness represented.

It may be appropriate then, at this critical juncture of Singapore's history, during which this year's government's budget has implicitly embraced a model of co-responsibility for what was previously a self-funded model of retirement savings, to explicitly create an integrated, unified platform for all future schemes to supplement the CPF. I call this platform, for lack of a better word, CPF-Plus. In other words, a "Big CPF" may be simpler and better than many small supplements.

On the other end of the spectrum, that of making babies, the central issue is whether we are prepared to take the perhaps radical steps which have enabled some developed Western countries to raise their birth rates from near terminal decline to more than replacement levels. Whether such steps, which largely involve creating a state-funded parental support eco-system, is prohibitively expensive or a vital necessity, depends on whether we consider our birth rate to be a strategic imperative of the same priority as say, National Service (NS), which is certainly not cheap either.

Let me now develop the framework for a discussion of CPF-Plus.

The optimistic Singapore narrative talks about our young grasping the future in their hands to decide our nation's destiny. But going by our rate of ageing, perhaps the real future is one of precipitous decline and a silver-haired or balding nation burdening the younger generation and grappling with its unpreparedness.

We're one of the fastest ageing countries in the world. Today only around 10% of Singaporeans and 25% of Japanese citizens are 65 years old or more. But around 40 years from now, within the timespan we are discussing, we will intersect with Japan and shortly thereafter we will overtake it. In other words, in the next 40 years, our elderly will triple in numbers — from one in 10 to one in three. That rate of ageing is unsurpassed in the world.

From Third to First World in a single generation, and then from Young to Old in another single generation.

The corollary problem with such rapid ageing is that retirement adequacy can only erode as time passes. The inevitable and inexorable trend is simply that, like chasing someone who is running even faster, life expectancy is extending faster than the age of retirement. Every generation is living longer and also retiring later, but the ratio of retirement

> **It may be appropriate then, at this critical juncture of Singapore's history, during which this year's government's budget has implicitly embraced a model of co-responsibility for what was previously a self-funded model of retirement savings, to explicitly create an integrated, unified platform for all future schemes to supplement the CPF. I call this platform, for lack of a better word, CPF-Plus.**

years to working years is not the same. The ratio is increasing in favour of retirement years, so that what we save in our working lives have to be stretched out over a longer period. The net effect is less money to spend each year.

When the CPF was created 60 years ago and retirement age was 55 years old, life expectancy was around 65 years old. This means that our parents worked during the first 85% of their lives (excluding of course non-working early years and other sources of income other than salaries) and their savings financed the remaining 15%. I call this 85:15 ratio the retirement funding ratio. A high ratio indicates a high probability of retirement adequacy, simply because there are more working years to build up savings for fewer retirement years. Conversely, a lower ratio means poorer retirement adequacy because fewer working years are available to finance a longer retirement period.

Now fast forward to 2015. Life expectancy is now around 82 years old and the retirement age has extended to 62 years old. The retirement funding ratio has now declined to 76:24. This will worsen to 72:28 when our children's life expectancy rise to say 92 years old and they retire at say 66 years old.

From a work-life balance perspective, this is social progress. Instead of retirement as a short precursor to death, we will enjoy longer, more active and meaningful retirement years. For our parents, 15% of their life expectancy could be enjoyed as retirement; for us it will be 24%, and for our children, up to 28%. And so it goes on with approximately three years of increased life expectancy every decade but perhaps half that in terms of retirement age. Eventually almost one-third of our life expectancy can be spent in retirement, and that will be double what the pioneer generation enjoyed. This seems to be great — social progress, active and happy retirement.

There is only one hitch: who's going to pay for all these golden years?

An enjoyable second career may be possible for professionals and other white collar workers, but for the bulk of the working class, post-retirement employment is usually part-time or at a lower wage, and is usually no less stressful than the first career. Exacerbating this is the fact that the cost of retirement rises faster than income from salaries.

So if the retirement funding ratio is not to worsen, people of my generation can stop working only at 70 years old and my children will have to retire at 78 years old. This may be physically possible and some may well choose to do so but they will have to sacrifice enjoying retirement or doing voluntary service.

In a collective social security system, the state pays for all the bonus years, and that's why in Western developed countries there is a concern that current generations have to fund future generations' hip operations and physiotherapy exercises. But because social security is collectivised, no single or individual pensioner is having anxiety attacks that his own state-funded pension will run out. In a self-funded compulsory savings system — which to me includes the employer's contribution because companies consider this to be part of an employee's total compensation cost — the anxiety is much higher, because you only have what you personally saved up to tide you into retirement.

And whilst this is good for the state and avoids inter-generational funding pressures, it puts the pressure squarely on the individual Singaporean.

Government's approach to this problem is to ring-fence the truly exorbitant post-retirement expenses from a person's retirement needs so that the monthly CPF pay outs can be quite small. And so, medical care for the most needy is heavily subsidised through Medifund; the elderly have their own special Pioneer Generation Package, and Medishield Life provides universal hospitalisation insurance.

Another potential drain on retirement adequacy is the cost of housing, which can be painful for low-income retirees who do not own their own homes. In Singapore this problem does not exist because of widespread home ownership, financed by CPF accounts.

But that still leaves the non-medical, non-housing costs of retirement spending. The fundamental dilemma of a worsening retirement funding ratio is simply that retirement adequacy will inevitably worsen over time. Furthermore, people's expectations of what basket of goods or services should constitute a minimally acceptable retirement lifestyle will only increase over time as we become more developed and affluent.

One argument has been that if people were willing to monetise their homes by selling and downgrading, or do reverse mortgages with the HDB, a lot of cash will be released for them to spend during retirement. The problem is that this option has not been popular at all in Singapore and most people seem to consider home ownership an essential part of their retirement security.

The anxiety of Singaporeans as they approach what should be the happiest period of their lives — an active, enjoyable retirement as the reward for all their hardwork-

> **Fifty years ago the social contract our pioneer leaders made with the people of Singapore through the CPF–HDB dual promise was instantly audacious, compelling, and risky in its promise.**

ing years — will not lessen but will instead increase, unless there is an explicit assurance that a fundamental change will be made to the current CPF model. And mind you, at 2,402.4 work hours a year, we already work the longest hours in the world.

Fifty years ago the social contract our pioneer leaders made with the people of Singapore through the CPF–HDB dual promise was instantly audacious, compelling, and risky in its promise. People rallied to its simplicity and the PAP's ability to deliver on this promise underpinned to a great extent, its continuing success at the polls.

Today, the original CPF vision has been tweaked almost beyond recognition and is unable to provide by itself, retirement adequacy for Singaporeans. The government has responded with laudable and socially beneficial schemes outside the CPF system, but the social compact which the CPF represented in its simplicity is at risk of being frayed because the uncertainties about retirement adequacy are being addressed by separately conceptualised and executed schemes.

To erase anxieties and restore the CPF as the cornerstone of our retirement system, is a simple, bold and audacious commitment now needed, for the next 50 years?

Should the state simply guarantee all Singaporeans that it will top up the accounts of those CPF members, plus citizens without CPF savings, to whatever levels are periodically deemed necessary by a competent authority for a minimally reasonable level of retirement livelihood? I note here that the commitment should not be limited to just a survival level of retirement livelihood, but to a reasonable level as determined by periodic and impartial assessment (such as by an advisory panel), because what constitutes reasonableness will change as we mature into an increasingly developed and affluent society.

This unequivocal commitment, with all schemes to be encompassed within the single CPF platform, is what I call CPF-Plus.

If for example a competent authority such as an advisory panel were to determine that the minimum monthly sum required for a basic but dignified retirement lifestyle for any particular period of years is say $1,000 a month, then the difference between that and what the Minimum Sum or Basic retirement Sum can provide, will come in the form of direct cash injections to that CPF account. The SSS is similar in concept, but is an independent scheme and until more financing and administrative details are revealed, it is hard to comment further.

CPF-Plus can be funded from the net investment income of our national reserves. This is the surplus generated by investing our reserves, after deducting for liabilities such as payment to CPF account holders. The Constitution was amended in 2008 to allow up to half of the Net Investment Returns (NIR) to be utilised by the government for current spending. To be cautious and to not have an open-ended commitment which it might regret later, the commitment could be capped at a certain percentage of NIR, such as 5% or 10% — whatever is both prudent as well as likely to be sufficient.

If even committing a maximum percentage of NIR to CPF-Plus is considered too radical, another option is to set up an endowment fund, which is only a once-off commitment, and allows increases to the fund to future governments to decide.

In this case only the investment returns from the endowment fund would be utilised for CPF-Plus. This is how Medifund is structured, and it has grown from S$200 million in 1993 to S$3 billion now. To put some figures in perspective, the current Silver Support Scheme (SSS) is going to cost $350 million a year. Say we establish an endowment fund and it manages to generate 4% profit. In order to get $350 million a year, there needs to be around $9 billion in the CPF-Plus endowment fund to begin start with.

Several basic principles should be adhered to for CPF-Plus.

First, it should be paid into the CPF accounts of only those Singaporeans whose retirement savings will not be adequate to fund their retirement needs, as determined periodically by a competent authority convened every say, four to five years. In other words, there should be a means test for reasons of social equity. This, of course, also assumes that the CPF will revert to its original role as a savings fund, so that people cannot intentionally draw down or overspend their CPF savings for housing or investments just in order to be topped up by CPF-Plus.

Second, it should take into account the fact that non-working Singaporeans do not even have CPF accounts but still need retirement savings. This can be a good opportunity to reform the present CPF-only-for-workers model entirely, so that husbands can pay part of their own CPF into their wives' accounts if they are home-makers or care-givers. Or, to go a step further, these home-makers or care-givers are given an allowance from the state, which goes into their CPF. One of the biggest irritations of people who do national income accounting, is that if you are a homemaker, you don't actually contribute to the economy, but if you hire a foreign domestic worker, that maid actually contributes to the economy. That is one anomaly that I think every working mother, despite generating the same amount of work at home, realises. Our CPF system also does not recognise this.

Third, it can be tweaked to reward those who are willing to save more, or willing to withdraw later, than the minimum mandated by CPF regulations, or even to reward entire special groups such as national servicemen.

Explicitly committing to a CPF-Plus co-responsibility model for retirement payment removes the anxiety from

> This can be a good opportunity to reform the present CPF-only-for-workers model entirely, so that husbands can pay part of their own CPF into their wives' accounts if they are home-makers or care-givers. Or, to go a step further, these home-makers or care-givers are given an allowance from the state, which goes into their CPF.

Singaporeans that occasional measures to help them may still not be enough to bridge future retirement funding gaps.

Furthermore, it also provides flexibility for a government because the cap on the NIR percentage to be used for CPF-Plus or the increase to the endowment fund, depending on which model is used, can be determined from time to time and, therefore, can be kept within the limits of sustainable and realistic long term investment returns from the reserves. This will minimise the likelihood of unfunded pension liabilities that haunt the pension systems of the developed world.

There may be two objections to CPF-Plus. First, to guarantee a supplemental source of funding for a person's CPF account may erode the work ethic and disincentivise savings. Second, drawing upon the reserves, even if only the Net Investment Returns (NIR), may slide us even further down the slippery slope of raiding the reserves, which started with the constitutional amendment to allow half the NIR to be used as current expenditure.

There are sound counter-arguments to these objections. To top up a person's CPF account just prior to retirement, whenever that is determined to be, does not equate to giving money to a person during his working years. Rewarding sections of the population through CPF-Plus does not erode the work ethic nor create an entitlement mentality of hand-outs because of its deferred impact. It can even be argued that such a scheme can help to inculcate a culture of deferred gratification.

The fact is that CPF-Plus is in line with values of governance in Singapore, which starting with the ideological origins of the People's Action Party (PAP), are more aligned towards social democracy than *laissez-faire* or market capitalism. And Singaporeans are better off for it.

Medifund, Workfare Income Supplement Scheme, or the Pioneer Generation Package have not eroded the work ethic nor created an entitlement mentality of hand-outs. They have rewarded and brought comfort to sections of the population.

As for drawing upon the net investment returns or NIR of the reserves to fund CPF-Plus, we need to recognise that not only is the NIR already being tapped for various purposes, but that this is not transferring the burden of funding CPF-Plus to future generations, which would be the case with most tax-based collective social safety nets.

Indeed, this may prompt a separate discussion on the reserves itself. The fact that the government amended the Constitution to allow half the NIR to be allocated for current expenditure implies a recognition that the growth of our reserves is approaching a point of sufficiency for whatever unforeseen contingencies may arise.

NIR should belong to current and not future generations, and failure to return at least a large chunk of such returns to finance a current generation's welfare is in fact, inter-generationally inequitable.

It can be argued that after this point is reached — whatever size of reserves it might imply — NIR should belong to current and not future generations, and failure to return at least a large chunk of such returns to finance a current generation's welfare is in fact, inter-generationally inequitable.

The case can even be made that as more pioneer Singaporeans who contributed to our reserves are dying out and as we multiply less, our reserves per capita increases at an exponential rate, and thus if anything, the government should consider being more generous with its spending. In any case, how much more of the NIR can be utilised rather than saved; for whatever purposes, and when, should all be a major part of our national conversation. In fact, the genie has been let out of the bottle once the constitutional amendment was made to allow 50 percent of NIR to be utilised. This debate needs to occur among Singaporeans because this is the source of both, on one hand, of our conservative retention of our safety net, but at the same time it is a source of spending, for a generation of people that perhaps deserve to have proper retirement adequacy.

After having dealt with retirement adequacy and old age, let me now move from the geriatric end of the spectrum to the very young — all those who are capable, but not producing babies.

The second issue is whether we as a society are willing to do what it seems to be required, to bring birth rates back to and even exceed replacement levels. Contrary to what we used to think some ten to 15 years ago, this clearly can and has been done, but the costs are not negligible.

Ever since the mid-1960's when the Government launched a population control program, our Total Fertility Rate (TFR) has been continually declining. For three decades our TFR has been below the replacement rate of 2.1 births per woman, and since 2003, a dozen years ago, it has been less than 1.3 births per woman. We're hovering at the edge of the precipice, the so-called the low-fertility trap, which is when a confluence of demographic, sociological and economic trends all converge and create a self-reinforcing, unstoppable spiral downwards. A slight uptick last year is encouraging news, but hardly a trend yet.

A few years ago our population already started to shrink, although it has not been noticeable to most people because of the influx of new citizens and Permanent Residents (PRs). Arresting this trend will not be easy: one IPS finding was that even with an increased TFR to say, 1.8 births per woman, which is quite optimistic and is 50% higher than at present, the resident population will still start to decline in the next 15–20 years.

We would need to take in about 20,000 new citizens per year on a net basis — meaning it has to be more in reality to offset those migrating out of Singapore — to stem the decline and achieve simple zero population growth. This is about the size of the Marine Parade HDB resident population each year. It is not small. And with anti-immigration sentiments persisting, if at least not increasing, in-migration cannot fill the population gap.

However, the demographic future of Singapore need not be as dismal as statistics suggest, nor should we be defeatist. Birth rates in developed countries have somehow bottomed out and are starting to increase again. Demographers have discovered that when the Human Development Index (HDI) increases, fertility rates decline, but reach a level where it becomes a J-curve and start to rise again. The HDI is a more holistic measure of development beyond simply economic wealth, which in my last lecture, I advocated that Singapore adopt.

The negative correlation between rising HDI and falling birth rates has been observed for decades and was once thought to be inevitable. After all, it was a trend with virtually every country observed — as lifestyles improve, parents want fewer children.

But a study, first published in the magazine *Nature* in 2009, found that at some point as the HDI continues to advance, meaning that as standards of living began to improve even further, people don't produce less children — fertility rates start to rise again. Some Western developed countries such as France, Sweden and Norway have seen fertility actually climbing back to replacement levels after decades of continuing decline. In the US, fertility briefly surged above replacement level and is now hovering around there. New Zealand's TFR is now at replacement level.

What has caused this reversal in birth rates, and how can it be sustained?

The prevailing theory is that this considerable and apparently sustained uptick in fertility rates is due to changing notions of gender-roles within the family, work-life balance within careers, and government policies which support the ability of families to enjoy the natural happiness of raising children.

Studies in Europe have shown that before 1985, as more women went to work, couples have fewer children. Singapore's history corroborates this trend. But after 1985, the correlation reversed — countries where more women worked started to gradually have higher birth rates than those where more women stayed home. This has noticeably not happened in Singapore where birth rates have stayed stubbornly low. Other East Asian countries like Hong Kong and Taiwan have similar trends to Singapore. Why is that so?

Sociologists say the data suggest that countries which recognise through concrete policies that young families today only want more children if both parents undertake equal responsibility for child rearing, and that children are well taken care of while both parents continue to engage in their careers, will get a positive response from young parents. In other words, there is no need for campaigns to encourage people to have at least one and preferably two children, or to bribe them with cash grants to make more babies.

A two-child — or more — family is a natural desire of parents, but they are not procreating because the overall

> A two-child — or more — family is a natural desire of parents, but they are not procreating because the overall support environment is not conducive. Create a truly conducive environment and leave the rest to nature.

support environment is not conducive. Create a truly conducive environment and leave the rest to nature.

In fact, there is a phenomena in the behavioural sciences called motivation crowding theory, which when applied would mean that trying to use money to motivate what should be an intrinsic desire — that of having children — can have the perverse effect of reversing the desired result instead. So creating a suitable environment (which cannot be monetised as easily) is much better than direct cash hand-outs for bearing children.

What might such an environment entail for us in Singapore? Well, such truly pro-family policies will not come cheap. Sweden grants each new parent two months of paid leave which cannot be transferred between each other, and another full year — 360 days — of leave which can be shared or transferred between themselves. Parents on leave are paid 80% of their monthly salary for 80% of the total leave allowable, with a cap which is roughly S$ 6,500. The balance 20% allowable leave is paid at a lower flat rate. So just as our state subsidises those who go back for their annual reservist training, the state can do likewise if we move in this direction.

This seems to have worked. Sweden's previously declining fertility rates have almost returned to replacement levels, and further refinements are likely to spur even higher growth.

One refinement is an interesting example of how family dynamics operate and how the state can nudge behaviour. Data showed that Swedish mothers used up on average 75% of their total leave entitlement, but fathers only 25% or two months, and pressured their wives to take up the majority of the shared leave.

This was resented and so the government — recognising who ultimately calls the shots when it comes to child birth — will reduce the shared leave and give more to the father so that the pressure will be on them to use it or lose it. The state essentially helped mothers to nudge fathers to do their share of parenting — which was a key factor in convincing women to have more children. That means for the young guys out there, the reason why we're not having more kids is because you're not helping out with the responsibility that comes with having more kids. That's only part of the story.

High quality and inexpensive child care facilities are also important and Sweden again leads in the provision of such services, even to the extent of having overnight centres for children of single parents who have to do shift work. Sweden is just one example; other European countries pursuing the same policies have achieved similar results.

The takeaway for Singapore is that if we want the same birth rates as in Europe, we should work harder to promote work-life integration and gender equality within the family, so that for women there is no trade-off between having a meaningful career and enjoying motherhood.

> **The takeaway for Singapore is that if we want the same birth rates as in Europe, we should work harder to promote work-life integration and gender equality within the family, so that for women there is no trade-off between having a meaningful career and enjoying motherhood.**

The Singapore government is well aware of the success of these European countries, whose experts have visited Singapore and shared their experiences. But there seems to be either scepticism about the impact of long parental leave on fertility rates, or an unwillingness to confront the economic costs of such programs. Employers, already reeling under the current clampdown on foreign workers, will be extremely unhappy about having to give a lot more paid leave to their child-bearing employees.

But as our fertility rates continue to plunge while Europe starts to see a reversal, it behooves us to perhaps consider whether the strategic dangers of not stemming a population decline may actually outweigh the economic costs.

We need to decisively conclude whether we are facing an issue of demographic security requiring the same kind of mind-set shift which enabled national service to be implemented, despite the loss of economic productivity as well as cost to the state.

Furthermore, we may have to change the entire support system for the young family, beyond just increasing paternity and maternity leave.

An entire eco-system of SMEs has to be created to undertake more of the work done by working parents. Liberalising the employment of domestic helpers will not necessarily help and there is even some evidence to suggest that it may be counter-productive. Young families with domestic maids have found themselves on one hand, increasingly dependent on them to relieve their stress, but without increasing the intimacy of family life to encourage more children.

We need a network of SMEs to which much housework, family meal preparation, and many other household chores can be outsourced. Reliable childcare facilities need to be more widespread, particularly in or near the workplace or home. This also creates the opportunity for an entire set of new SMEs to populate our economic landscape, and give job opportunities for all our young entrepreneurs. In fact, for those who think that this kind of expenditure is overdone, there's been a recent MIT study to show that every dollar spent on early childcare and early child education, actually saves 13 dollars in total cost to the state later on in the development of that person. Facilities and services serving the dependents of young working families — both the aged and the infants — will also go a long way to encourage Singapore families to want to enjoy having rather than being stressed by, more children.

But unless we recognise that our current policies are not working and learn from other countries which have indeed achieved success, we will simply go into genteel decline and bemoan our fate, whilst not doing much about it.

Before I wrap up, just a few words on the notion of the family. While it may be an exaggeration to say that the traditional family is under assault in the West by new trends such as single parenthood, same-sex marriages with adopted children, unmarried parents, and short-lived marriages, alternatives to the traditional nuclear family are certainly growing.

For many years, the Singapore policy of being pro-family meant active discouragement of whatever lifestyles were considered not pro-family, to the extent that single parents or unmarried singles, found it difficult to access state-funded benefits such as public housing. Insofar as the goal of an inclusive society, to which we are committed, means that all Singaporeans are equally entitled to state protection and assistance, we do need to be more tolerant towards alternative family norms, whilst not undermining the fundamental nuclear family model.

In conclusion, the demographic shape of Singapore is changing very rapidly and the society our children will inherit may not even be recognisable to us today. The twin challenges of providing retirement adequacy and encouraging a replacement-level birth rate, may require paradigm shifts in thinking. Inevitably there will be trade-offs, for no solution is ever completely cost-free. The discussion for these trade-offs, however, needs to be had openly, and as soon as possible.

We need to debate new ideas and assume that everything is do-able unless otherwise proven, rather than immediately reject anything new as not-doable unless proven otherwise. I found out that in brainstorming sessions, putting the burden of proof on the naysayers is a good way to encourage the flow of new ideas. This means to say that everything is doable unless it is proven otherwise, rather than everything is not doable unless you prove it can be done.

I hope to have contributed to this debate through a few suggestions made possible by this lecture series. But I hope that more suggestions will be forthcoming and that our leaders in the policy formulation corridors of ministries or parliament will not dismiss ideas from all of us as out of hand, or as un-informed and irresponsible ones. An active citizenry is about embarking on a process of enquiry to assess what works for the future of Singaporeans. I think it behooves all of us to have the courage to make suggestions which may be laughed at, but for you to make it, because only then, will we achieve the civil society that we seek.

My next lecture will be my final one. It will be on the most amorphous and the most challenging topic: "Society and Identity", and will be held on April 9. And I think that Society and Identity is probably the most important issue we face, as a society and as a people, going forward.

I have learnt, in the course of four lectures so far, how much I do not know through this journey, and hope to share some of that ignorance with you then.

Thank you and have a good evening ahead.

Questions and Answers
Moderator: Dawn Yip

Question: You mentioned that Western countries are reversing the decline in their Total Fertility Rate (TFR). In Western countries, it is also more common now for couples to live together, have kids, and then get married. Do you think this would happen in Singapore? What are the institutional barriers that prevent this from happening?

Ho Kwon Ping (HKP): I don't believe we're currently seeing this trend in Singapore, or in East Asia as a whole, where people shun marriage and live together and produce children. There is a trend, more than before, of unmarried people living together. Most of the time when they decide to have children, they'll get married.

I referred to alternative family norms in my lecture because if these do arise in Singapore, we should recognise these trends, not necessarily to encourage them, but not to actively discourage them. If that becomes the way of the world and more and more people want to live together, lead very happy lives together, have civil unions without the religious sacrament of marriage, then personally I think that the state should recognise that. In doing so, we would have more children also.

My only disquiet about people living together, who are not married, is that this often is at the disadvantage to the female partner who may not recognise this early on in life but later on it can really badly affect them. So I do believe that the institution of a civil union where rights are accorded to people in a marriage is important for the protection of both parties in a union.

Question: Do you think that Singapore saves too much both collectively as a nation as well as individually?

HKP: It's an interesting question, particularly at the national level. It is fully understandable in terms of our psyche towards the welfare state. We in Singapore have been particularly averse to the welfare state because we've seen the excesses of welfarism and the problematic legacies it imposes on future generations. As a nation, we've felt our vulnerability and hence, we feel the necessity of building up the reserves. This was very understandable, and absolutely necessary for the first 50 years of Singapore's history. But I think the debate on whether we are saving too much does have to start now.

The issue is: How much is enough conceptually, without going into absolute numbers? And how much reserves accumulation is enough before you can start to spend the income from it? This debate started in 2008 and now it's actually becoming a public issue. It's a healthy discussion. State-funded welfare was always seen as the slippery slope and we have gone the other way of saving too much. There are lessons we can glean from negative experiences in the West so that as we spend more now — which I think we should — we do not need to go the whole hog and we can avoid the mistakes that have plagued quite a number of countries in the West, which they're regretting.

Question: Young people feel that rising costs and the demands of the education system are affecting how they feel about having children. I would hazard a guess that some of this is due to the expectations that parents have. Another is the long hours we work. You need time and leisure to make babies. Should there be legislation where employers would be penalised if their employees would stay beyond a certain number of hours?

HKP: There is absolutely no assurance, that if employees are forced to leave their workplace, that they are necessarily going home to make babies. You may find that the pubs of Singapore will be very full. On the serious side, I think the problem of low fertility is a complex one. My understanding is that the natural desire to have children is very strong amongst young people, but it is the immediate pressures within the first few years, that of career advancement and work life balance, that is difficult to achieve if one wants to start a family. It's not just the government's role; it's attitudes between couples themselves as well.

Question: We actually already are tapping Net Investment Returns (NIR) on our reserves for the Budget. So really, the question then is, how much of NIR do you want to spend?

HKP: We need this debate very much because previously, anyone who suggested drawing down our NIR would be told that they're a liberal and that suggestion wouldn't go very far. The People's Action Party (PAP) government has itself has started doing it[1] since 2008 and I think the NIR has been used to finance some extremely good programmes. All I'm saying is that we are ready right now to have a discussion on how much should be used. I'm not in any disagreement with any what's happening, I think it's very healthy, but it's not been part of discussions Singaporeans have.

Question: First: The reality is that most low-income workers have unfairly experienced not being paid Central Provident Fund (CPF). They are caught in the daily grind and may not pursue what is actually their right, because there are studies that show that if you are in chronic poverty, you have a short-term outlook and may not think about long-term implications.

Second: The cost of retirement has become higher and the government is doing what it can to address that. Then, for TFR to rise, we need

---

[1] The Constitution was amended in 2008 to apply the NIR framework to the Monetary Authority of Singapore (MAS) and GIC. Under the NIR framework, the Government can spend up to 50% of the long-term expected real returns (including capital gains) on assets managed by MAS and GIC, minus the liabilities of the Government and MAS.

high-quality childcare services. There are policies to ensure child care is affordable. Should the government nationalise or take back more sectors from private sector, so that the cost of living can be tempered?

HKP: Yes, but to a very limited extent. We need to recognise that the nationalisation of too many services can also result in a high level of inefficiency. From a purely economic argument: One should look at what are the natural monopolies that already exist. These should be owned by the government and with services provided subsidised. In the case of Mass Rapid Transit (MRT) operator SMRT Corporation Ltd. all the heavy investments are already funded by the state, it's only the rolling stock that is owned by SMRT. SMRT, being largely government-owned, is already a nationalised entity. The problem is that it has been told to play within the rules of the market place, so it has to make profits and perhaps therein is the problem that expenses go up too high. So I would agree that certain services should be reconsidered, but it should be on a very selective basis.

On vulnerable groups who don't have CPF — yes, the lower your income is, the more unlikely you're going to be aware of the plethora of schemes out there that can help you. That's why we have quite an opportunity to keep CPF as the simple system by which government supplements are issued. We need to look at this category of workers who for various reasons don't have enough CPF for retirement and see if they can receive injections to their accounts. So that if you are a working mother, home carer, or if you are an odd job labourer, you still have some CPF funds, allowing the CPF to be a fundamental safety net.

LECTURE V

SOCIETY AND IDENTITY

Good evening and welcome to the fifth and final lecture in the IPS — Nathan Lectures series.

In the last two weeks, the unprecedented and spontaneous outpouring of grief and gratitude at the death of Mr Lee Kuan Yew has been a national catharsis. We have learnt that even in his passing, Mr Lee's final contribution was to bring all of us together in ways never done before, to realise that in our grieving, we rediscover our common identity.

And so it is perhaps fitting that the topic of this final lecture in the IPS-Nathan Lectures series is "Society and Identity". Our sense of nationhood has never been stronger than in the past weeks. When the fighter jets soar overhead and the national anthem is played on August 9, that lump in our throats will tell us who we are: One people, One nation, One Singapore.

But is it possible to more specifically define our identity, besides knowing that we have one? I jotted down a few sentences and asked some friends to identify the country which I described as follows:

> *We are an immigrant society, and, therefore, persistence and resilience are the hallmarks of our identity. We've been open to the world, but in recent years have turned more inwards and even somewhat hostile*

towards foreigners. We take pride in our egalitarian ethos, even though income inequality is worsening. We squabble amongst ourselves, but to foreigners we close ranks. We have a can-do attitude which can be perceived as being arrogantly proud of our exceptionalism. We tout our meritocracy as a core value even though it is starting to fray. Above all, we love to celebrate ourselves and our achievements, and how the best is yet to be.

Who are we?

The Singaporeans I asked unanimously said, of course that's us, Singaporeans.

Interestingly, another group I asked replied: of course you're describing our USA and the values behind our American Dream.

So here you have two countries, worlds apart almost in every possible way, from population and geographic size to historical origins; from political and social culture to current and future challenges; and yet the American Dream and the Singapore Dream are almost interchangeable.

Upon reflection, that is not so strange. After all, once you strip a Dream of its specific cultural context, many societies aspire for largely the same things in life. The common element between the American and Singapore Dreams is simply that both societies are audacious, brash, and young enough to believe that whoever you are, and wherever you come from, this is your land of opportunity. This is where you can achieve your personal and family dreams, and pursue a life of meaning and purpose.

But this is more the immigrant's Dream of Singapore than the Singaporean's Dream nowadays, simply because many citizens do not now feel that they can achieve anything if only they just tried. Yet, it is crucial to Singapore's continuing survival and well-being to maintain, nurture, and polish this Dream, both in terms of keeping its borders open to the outside world, as well as maintaining social mobility within.

So, in tackling this final lecture, I want to ask a simple question: How do we maintain the Singapore Dream as a meaningful, purposeful aspiration for all Singaporeans for the next 50 years? What are the most critical things we must do to overcome future or already-emerging challenges to this Dream?

After some deliberation I've consolidated the various challenges and must-do's into three major, over-arching tasks. They are:

- first, to strengthen the cohesive diversity which underpins our identity, against a climate of increasingly narrow rigidity;

- second, to improve social mobility and a culture of egalitarianism, in the midst of a fraying meritocracy and worsening income inequality; and

- third, to build a collaborative governance style and an information-rich civil society.

Let me now deal with each of these.

First, strengthening cohesive diversity. Our immigrant origins have created mechanisms for harmonious racial and religious co-habitation, but the traditional fault lines which were successfully held together, are facing un-familiar, non-traditional pressures which may result in new cracks.

There is increasingly vocal social diversity from people of different LGBT affiliations, or alternative family norms such as single or unmarried parents, or same-sex couples. In addition there is increasing intra-ethnic diversity from immigrants or foreign workers who may belong to the same race as defined by our traditional CMIO (Chinese-Malay-Indian-Other) categories — but hardly identify or socialise with each other. For example, new residents from China, Taiwan, and Hong Kong all form their own cliques which also largely exclude the Singaporean Chinese. The same is true or even more fragmented for South Asians, whether foreign workers or new citizens.

At another level, the Housing & Development Board (HDB) heartland world-view, with its *kopitiams* and *roti-prata* stalls, is being assailed by the slick and slightly intimidating

In other words, race and class and a consensus on social issues are becoming increasingly complex and intertwined in Singapore.

globalisation represented by Marina Bay Sands and "Billionaire's Cove" in Sentosa. In other words, race and class and a consensus on social issues are becoming increasingly complex and intertwined in Singapore.

The average Singaporean is anxious and confused by this onslaught of what is becoming a divisive diversity. That anxiety — what social psychologists call cognitive dissonance when reality increasingly diverges from our expectations — arises when the traditional racial lens of CMIO or the traditional norms of heterosexual orientation, what social scientists call hetero-normativity, a big word, no longer seem adequate to describe a rapidly changing Singapore society.

One way to resolve cognitive dissonance is to abandon our stereotyped presumptions and expectations and simply treat people as individuals and not categories. We should consciously blur or even abolish the CMIO model's simplistically rigid racial categories, and welcome the multiple identities and more complex sub-ethnicities which is increasingly the real Singapore of today.

The CMIO model, created out of necessity in the aftermath of a racially charged road to independence, has helped to create common ground between those of different tongues and dialects, but it also has the effect of oversimplifying the diversity that is our social mix. How we define people often shapes how they behave, so the less we pigeon-hole people, the more chances we have for a cohesive diversity. Just thinking about a post-CMIO model already seeds a future paradigm shift.

Singapore is ethno-culturally more similar to New York City than to the homogeneity of Tokyo or Shanghai. The hallmark of New York's success is that so many culturally traditional or ethnically specific neighbourhoods can co-exist cheek by jowl, and even next to skyscraper icons of global capitalism. What seems to be totally unplanned and therefore chaotic has its own logic: because there are no rigid expectations, there is no clash with reality and therefore no cognitive dissonance. Everyone is unique, everyone is quirky, everyone

> **How we define people often shapes how they behave, so the less we pigeon-hole people, the more chances we have for a cohesive diversity.**

is rude and kind at different times, and everyone has to simply respect and even appreciate the other's difference.

This genuine form of cohesive diversity is messy, dynamic and defies classification, but New Yorkers, for all their amazing diversity, all love their city. Like New Yorkers, Singaporeans must also embrace each other as individuals and not as categories along the CMIO model. Without stereotypical expectations we can accept and appreciate each person as different but from whom we can learn new things. In a post-CMIO model people will have more time and space to replace old stereotypes with more nuanced complexities, reflected in more varieties of socio-ethnic identities. This is a strategic imperative not just for enriching the Singapore identity, but to continually attract the world's best talent and make this island, in the words of PM Lee, "the best city to live, work, and play".

Another way to strengthen cohesive diversity is for the majority race in Singapore to consciously overcome what one insightful blogger has called the mindset of Chinese Privilege, which is the attitude of a majority race towards minorities where it does not see itself as racist but acts on assumptions which are based on privileges which only it can have as the majority race. It can manifest in small ways, such as speaking in the majority-race language even when foreigners are part of the gathering, or making jokes which are racial slurs but justifying them because they were light-hearted and not malicious.

A final building block for cohesive diversity is recognition of the marginalised people whom my research assistant Andrew Yeo compared to the composer Claude Debussy's famous dictum that "music is the space between the notes", meaning that there is equal importance in what is unseen or unheard. It is the voices of the foreign worker, the single mum, and the many other silent spaces between our national notes which make

It is the voices of the foreign worker, the single mum, and the many other silent spaces between our national notes which make our Singapore song complete and more interesting.

our Singapore song complete and more interesting. Even though they are neither citizens nor permanent residents, the 1.5 million "permanently transient" semi-skilled foreign workers and domestic helpers cannot be an invisible community overlaying the visible Singapore, with uneasy points of contact which can become flashpoints. A society measured by the height of its skyscrapers and size of its shopping malls is in my view, the ultimate Dubai-style dystopia; far better that we measure ourselves by how we treat the marginalised and voiceless in our midst.

As the cacophony of strident voices increase in the future — the gays against the anti-gays; the born-again Christians against everyone else; the PRC Chinese against the "*suaku*" local Singaporean, the elite Delhi-born immigrant against his uncouth Tamil neighbour — and the people in the silent spaces between the notes struggle to even make a small sound, we should not be worried, and should perhaps even pause to listen. It is just a new Singapore song in the making, not commissioned for a famous performer to sing, but created by the people themselves, from the ground up.

Second, improving social mobility and the egalitarian ethos. The path to success in Singapore has largely been through academic merit in transparent national examinations. That is the basis of what we call Singaporean meritocracy, which has its philosophical roots in Confucianism and its organisational principles in Imperial China's elite class of scholar-bureaucrats. The model has served us well in our early years.

But having already achieved the 50 year continuous growth from third world to first — over time the Singapore model is in danger of being a static meritocracy, which sieves people based on only a narrow measure of capability in single snapshots of time — examination results basically — and from thereon creates a self-perpetuating elite class. Ironically, the original social leveller and purest form of Singapore-style meritocracy — our educational system — may perpetuate inter-generational class stratification rather than level the playing field.

The warning signs are clear:

- Only 40% of the students in the most prestigious primary schools live in HDB flats, in contrast with 80% of all primary school students residing in HDB flats.

- More than half of PSC scholarship recipients live in private housing, compared with only 15% of the general population. And 60% of PSC scholars come from only two schools — Raffles Institution (Junior College) (RJC) and Hwa Chong Institution.

- 63% of university-educated fathers, 37% of those with secondary school qualifications, and only 12% of fathers with primary education or less, had children with university degrees.

No doubt, the index for social mobility is still higher in Singapore than in many other countries, including some of the famously egalitarian Nordic countries. This is comforting but no reason for complacency, especially against a background of worsening income inequality globally.

Some people have advocated that the way to redress structural inequality is to practise affirmative action for the disadvantaged group; for example, to give bonus examination points to any student whose parents did not attain university education. This would, however, be the start of an unending process of affirmative actions which will only demean and discredit our meritocracy in the long run. I believe that further reforms of the overall education system can promote social levelling without under-mining the principles of meritocracy nor the academic rigor for which Singapore is so well known. Let me share some of these possible measures with you:

- Ending pre-teen streaming and the Primary School Leaving Examination (PSLE) exams, and having all schools teach children a continuous ten years straight through to Secondary Four, so that less academic pressure early on in life allows more time for teachers to focus on the personal development of students, which has been found to have a great influence on later academic achievements.

- Giving admissions priority on the basis of distance from homes has to also be relooked, because the most prestigious and elite schools are also located in the most wealthy parts of the island. The handful of top primary schools have five-year waiting lists and parents or their maids queue overnight to get a place for their children. We must not forget that when the PAP came to power it took the then radical step of essentially nationalising the entire educational system, in order to achieve its then socialist goals. Similarly radical steps need to be at least discussed, if not immediately adopted.

- Replacing the rigid, narrowly-directed with a far broader, multifaceted program which focusses on the special needs of all students, whether it be due to special talents in the arts or sciences or other academic areas, or special disabilities such as mild autism or dyslexia. There has been much talk that education must now aim to develop the full potential of every student. It is time to walk the talk. Schools in a geographic cluster can specialise in their own areas of excellence, and serve special-needs students from that cluster, whether the special needs are special talents or disabilities.
- Examples of other easier and simpler programs include: providing student counselling services in every school, because disproportionately more students from lower-income and less-educated families have emotional and domestic problems which inhibit their academic performance; or introducing volunteer tuition services by university students for secondary schools, as part of mandatory community service modules in all our universities, which will help students who cannot afford expensive private tutors. Yet another idea which is already starting to happen, is the rotation of top principals and teachers into neighborhood schools. All these and other piecemeal measures with the same intent, can add up to create a powerful overall impact.

Besides reforms to the educational system, the civil service needs to also lead in social levelling. Recent announcements that non-graduates will be allowed to fill positions previously eligible only for graduates is a good start. But only if the most elite cadre of civil servants — the Administrative Service — changes its recruitment criteria to create an open and level playing field, can we start to have a continuous, dynamic meritocracy where one's destiny is not already largely determined at 12 years old, reinforced at 18, and virtually fixed at 22.

Third, building a collaborative governance style and an information-rich civil society. When I first entered university some 40 plus years ago, the target of student activism was an obscure Latin expression, "*In Loco Parentis*" — which is a legal doctrine whereby certain institutions such as universities, actually assume the legal powers of a parent.

The Singapore state has not assumed the same level of paternalism over its citizens, but it has come close, making decisions which might elsewhere be individual responsibilities. Whilst this has been widely accepted in the past 50 years, a paternalistic governance culture may need to change to a collaborative model in the future. This is already happening with the abundance of debate about directions facing Singapore in the post-LKY era. However, such a governance culture of participatory democracy can only work if the institutions of civil society can be actively engaged in decision-making.

For that to happen, Civil society players need access to that lifeblood of robust discussion: freely available and largely unrestricted information. Information is the oxygen without which civil society players suffocate in their own ignorance and resort only to repetitive drumming of their causes, but without the ability to really engage with their own members, with other players, or with government. Access to information is an existential imperative for civil society to perform its functions responsibly and knowledgeably.

The currently unequal access to information is called by academics, "information asymmetry" and one of the reasons all governments are averse to sharing information is not just because of the sensitivity of secrets, but because information is power, and asymmetry between seeker and owner of information shapes their relative power relationship.

To rectify this imbalance, some civil society activists have called for a Freedom of Information Act (FOIA). This would require open access to and declassification of all government archives after 25 to 30 years, and almost unfettered access to information about oneself at any time.

So should Singapore simply adopt FOIA? Just joining the bandwagon is not by itself meaningful. Of the 99 countries which have FOIA legislation are such beacons of liberal democracy as Nigeria, Uganda, Zimbabwe, China, Pakistan, Thailand, Russia, Yemen, and all the "-Stans" of

> **Civil society players need access to that lifeblood of robust discussion: freely available and largely unrestricted information.**

Central Asia. The reputation of these countries for good governance are so questionable that one must wonder whether their own FOIA are actually devices to smoke out and track potential dissidents.

Of course, most Western liberal democracies do have effectively functioning FOIA, but while it has redressed information asymmetry, the downside is that it also exacerbates the adversarial relationship between civil society and government. Whilst this may be the underlying basis for a check and balance system in Western political cultures, it does not encourage a collaborative governance style. It can even be dysfunctional for the conduct of diplomacy and general statecraft, which must often require total confidentiality between parties. Just witness Hillary Clinton and the whole debacle about her private email system, which was her response to unfettered access of all government information in the United States by citizens.

One possible way to redress information asymmetry within a collaborative governance culture is to legislate a Code on Information Disclosure which is not legally enforceable but morally binding, and sets out the principles by which ministries can or should not protect information, and the importance of open sharing of information for a civil society. Ministries would be required to employ independent Access-to-Information Officers such as retired judges, to evaluate and give written replies to information requests. Media attention and public pressure would serve as leverage in cases of non-compliance with the Code, or where there is controversy. Hong Kong, I understand, has a system similar to what I have described, and it may behoove us to study that with more depth.

But with more information equality, there will inevitably be more and different interpretations of data, of events, of history itself. Official narratives, such as the controversies surrounding Operation Coldstore, will be questioned and debated by generations of new historians. The young possess a certain oddly dispassionate objectivity towards history compared to many of us for whom the past 50 years was filled with deep emotion and very personal partisan perspectives. The young don't take our version of history as the gospel truth; they want to discover the facts themselves and make up their own minds. This is healthy, because the attribute of critical enquiry and continual search for the truth, will stand the next generation in good stead as they transit to becoming the leadership generation.

Rather than consider such re-assessments of history to be revisionism which has to be prevented, we should accept that information equality will inevitably lead to such questioning. But we should also have confidence that history, through the collective wisdom of time and millions of people past, present and future, will accurately and fairly assess the enormous contributions and legacies of our past leaders, including Mr Lee Kuan Yew. We should trust in our young people enough to allow space for them to develop their own opinions. In the end, our future leaders of Singapore should be bold enough to own the future rather than simply defend the past.

History comprises both the universally experienced, historically momentous events and the small, personal milestones of each person. In this way, SG50 is a special year of meaning for me because on one hand, whilst we collectively commemorate our 50 years of independence and simultaneously mourn the death of the first and last of our founding fathers, I shall also celebrate the arrival of my first grandchild. Such is the cycle of life, of persons dying and babies being born.

My grandson, who will be 50 when Singapore celebrates its 100th anniversary, can only say he was born a few months after Mr Lee passed away. But even for my children, who are young adults, Mr Lee was always more a legend than a real person. Few young people today have ever known him other than as the textbook father of independent Singapore. My eldest son's only memory of Mr Lee was when he and his wife visited my family on the funeral of my father, some 16 years ago when Ren Hua was only a teenager and Mr Lee was already 75 years old.

When I was detained by Mr Lee under the ISA I was only 24 and he was already 53 years old — in his fearsome, intimidating prime of his life. When I joined the board of GIC, which he chaired, I was 44 and he was 72; when he inaugurated SMU's Ho Rih Hwa Lecture series, named after my father, I was 50 and he was nearing 80. Such is the age gap that most of the people who worked with him have passed on and those who worked directly under him have long retired. To the extent that in our initial years Singapore was almost synonymous with Lee Kuan Yew, he defined our national identity and we looked towards him for signals on how to behave, to think, to view ourselves. He said Rugged Society, and that was our identity during my generation's youth. As nation-building gained traction and we started to embrace ourselves as a people, a society, and a nation, we started to experiment with our own personal markers of identity. Today, I daresay Singapore comprises multiple identities.

We commonly describe a national identity as something constructed from tangible markers such as Singlish or durian or chicken rice, or intangible values such as pragmatism or tolerance, or whatever. If we put that all together to sculpt a single, proverbial Merlion identity, I think it will be iconic and recognisable more to foreigners than to us. The Merlion, I think, we have never really adopted as our identity because it is artificial, and any identity is not a static snapshot of a people, frozen in time.

It is a continual and never-ending work in progress of an evolving people. Our identity may have started more as a *rojak* salad than as an artificial Merlion but over time even the *rojak* salad will evolve further, with new and unusual ingredients. While the Merlion remains an un-natural and static animal.

Identity is what you are attached to, what you would fight for, what you care about. In a previous lecture, I proposed that we develop a uniquely Singaporean Human Development Index which would measure our overall 'wellbeing', besides only having GDP as an indicator. These intangible markers which measure our progress as a nation, will in part also form our identity, because it will give heft and weight and shape to what we value. We must put in place a framework for this fluid discussion to take place, to be mapped and to be expressed.

Whilst Singapore's identity is rooted in its immigrant heritage, and that open-ness should always be a cornerstone of our sense of self and underpin our receptivity towards those from other cultures, we should not feel lost if we are not able to define a single common identity. We are all identities in creation, and the end result will not be uniform. Instead, by sharing stories of who we are, we find resonance with

Identity is what you are attached to, what you would fight for, what you care about.

each other. These collective stories can kindle of sense of "being Singaporean", even if we cannot articulate or pin down specifics.

And so I'd like to close not by defining the Singapore identity, but by simply sharing with you my personal journey as a migrant to these shores. My father was a fourth-generation Singaporean, with his forefathers working as boat-builders in Tanjong Rhu. They built the *tong-kangs* or deep-bottomed bumboats and barges which ferried goods and people between Singapore and the hundreds of ships which made Singapore the pre-eminent port in Asia since several hundred years ago.

But I was not born here, did not study nor live here. I received my naturalised citizenship by a technicality — because my father was ambassador of Singapore to Thailand and our home since childhood became technically, sovereign Singapore territory. So for several years as a teenager I raised the flag every morning at our hastily erected flagpole on technically Singapore soil, and eventually I qualified to be a citizen. But my first extended stay in Singapore, for more than a week or so at a time, was at the age of 20 when I came here for National Service. Not ever having lived here, I wanted to see what it was like to be a Singaporean.

During National Service (NS) I was taunted by some as "*jiak kantang*" which means "eat-potato" and is a derogatory term for someone who has lost his roots and apes the West — much like a banana in Asian–American slang. Though I can do a decent Singlish by now, my natural accent is between English and American, and my Mandarin has no dialect overtones.

Although I studied at Taiwanese and American universities, I finally graduated from a Singapore university. So what is my identity? I'm not sure; and I will always remember that Mr Lee Kuan Yew once told me to my face that the only smart thing I ever did was to marry a Singaporean because he was wise to know that through Claire, I would find a sense of home.

I have lived and worked in this country since 1972: altogether 43 years. I met my wife here, my children were all born and grew up here. My simple answer as to why I chose to live and put down my roots here, is that here I do not feel a stranger. In Thailand where I spent my childhood I spoke Thai but was always an outsider. In Taiwan and in America I learnt much and made good friends, but I was a stranger in a strange land. However, Singapore's multitude of races and cultures made me feel no longer alien. Perhaps that is also what makes other new migrants decide to settle in Singapore — the fact that they could create their own identities here.

An open-ness and acceptance of foreigners — and indeed, of other Singaporeans who may be different from the mainstream in various ways — can perhaps become a defining characteristic of our identity. We can create our own identities even as we inherit certain common characteristics.

Singapore is my home because whoever I was, or am now, or want to be, I feel I can be that person here. However, this statement of pride is not universal. I am fortunate because I am a privileged, Chinese, heterosexual, male businessman. Can other persons, whose music is the silent spaces between the notes, also believe what I just said, so that we can honestly declare that cohesive diversity — this delightful oxymoron — is the unique marker of the Singapore identity? For the sake of the next 50 years, I fervently hope that we can, and will.

I now come to the end of my journey, a humbling exercise in discovering my own ignorance as I tried to speak on a wide range of topics. It has been almost one year since I was asked to be the first S R Nathan Fellow, and six months since the first lecture. I shall henceforth forfeit my title as temporary professor — my life goal — and return my faculty card to the NUS Registrar, and hope my Singapore Management University (SMU) colleagues welcome me back. And I can finally return to my favourite past time, as some of you have known, of watching consecutive and quite forgettable movies on long haul flights.

I would like to thank several people during the past few months.

First, to IPS: its Director my old friend Mr Janadas Devan, who was not completely honest when he said that this would be a simple thing you could do in your spare time. I would like to thank the Committee for the S R Nathan Fellowship for the Study of Singapore for making me their first victim, and Mr S R Nathan, who took the risk of asking me to be the first S R Nathan Fellow, despite my lack of academic credentials and my reputation — quite undeserved of course — for always putting my foot in my mouth. Thank you for your trust and I hope I have not dishonoured you. Good luck to the next victim … I mean the next Fellow.

To my research assistant, Andrew Yeo, thank you for being available 24/7 and for passing on many of the quite scatological and almost defamatory comments about me on social media after each lecture.

Andrew is a poster boy of the new Singaporean success story: poor student in a neighbourhood school, failed his Poly exams, clawed his way into a SIM distance learning university, but did so well that London School of Economics accepted him for a Master's degree in social policy. In my view, IPS is lucky to have him and he will be a real asset wherever he goes. And I am proud that at least in Singapore, we do have an open enough system, and we do have young people who are not the paragons of typical success stories, and Andrew truly has my respect for that.

To my children, all five of them, thank you for organising get-togethers with your peers so that I can understand how younger people feel about things, and not pretend that I am a young person. As only you know, everything that we do together as a family brings us that much closer and stronger, and the dinner conversations where you all gave your views, have contributed much. To my fiercest critic, strongest supporter and best friend: my wife Claire, thank you in particular for never mincing your words.

And finally, to the many of you whom I reached out to during these months for your views, who read and commented on the lectures, and whose views I may have shamelessly borrowed, or who wrote to me after attending a lecture or reading an essay — thank you so much for being part of this journey. Just simply knowing that all of us are out there, each trying in our own ways to make this a better Singapore — is very comforting.

Over the past half year I have put forth a range of ideas, some possibly crazy and some possibly workable. I hope I have not offended anyone and I apologise if I have. The ideas themselves are not that important. What I hope to have done, however, and which I hope will last long after tonight, is to encourage people to think their own thoughts and put them out there in the marketplace of ideas, so that in this messy exchange of voices and opinions, we all learn something from each other.

In the next 50 years — the Singapore after Mr Lee Kuan Yew — the line between leader and follower will start to blur; we will not just be disciplined and unquestioning followers. Our leaders will walk amongst and not ahead of us; they will be part of, and not simply lead, the national conversation. Other people may march to their own drumbeat and at their own pace. We may look from the outside, to be less orderly and consensual than in the past. After all, civil society is not a disciplined army; it is not an organised orchestra producing the soothing melodies of a lovely symphony. It is a loud cacophony of voices, of disorganised aspirations, of an exciting market place of ideas.

But I certainly hope that what will never change from one generation to another, is the passion to make this country continue to succeed, to be proud of who we have been, are, and will be, and to revel in the cohesive diversity that makes us all Singaporeans — whatever that word may mean to each of us.

The 13th century Persian poet Rumi once wrote something which should speak to each of us. He wrote,

"You are not a drop in the ocean. You are the entire ocean, in a drop."

In other words, you and I are not cogs in a machine, or grains of sand, or drops in the ocean. In each of us is the whole of Singapore. Each of us represents the collective identities and histories which make up our ocean and on which we shall continue our journey together.

Goodnight, and thank you for the pleasure of your company over the past months. It has been an immense privilege.

Questions and Answers

Moderator: Janadas Devan

Question: You have described Singapore's existing and emerging diversities. What do you think would be the main fault lines over the next 50 years?

Ho Kwon Ping (HKP): My sense is that the most important fault line that can re-emerge is if a future government tries to establish the primacy of a particular ethnic group through the primacy of a particular language or a particular religion. We've seen what's happened in Sri Lanka, where Tamils and Singhalese co-existed for generations. The introduction of Singhalese as the official language changed things. It was a clear signal that one race had to be the dominant one.

I'm advocating that the four broad categorisations of Chinese-Malay-Indian-Other (CMIO) be blurred further so that we have a greater diversity, but it must be a diversity where there is no dominant race that establishes itself simply because it is numerically dominant and hence superior in terms of language or religion. We've seen that happen elsewhere and it's not impossible that that could happen in Singapore again.

Question: First, regardless of how we try to impose social structures on identities, many social experiments demonstrate that people have natural affinities to their in-groups. Second, you've proposed tactical initiatives to improve our education system. Are you suggesting that we need to diminish the benefit of inherited advantages for children here?

HKP: I agree with your first comment that you can't change human nature. People would find affinity amongst people of their own kind, whatever that kind might be. All I'm simply saying is that I think we should try to, more consciously, break down barriers in order to allow people to have more cross-cultural communications. On education, I think I need to make clear that I'm commenting on aspects of how the education system, such as school admissions, is structured that have not helped to make education the great social leveller that it could be.

The points I have made in my lecture are not exhaustive and are from an amateur. The measures I proposed don't require spending more money. A lot of the restructuring that I think Singapore society should go through in the next 50 years is not a matter of reallocating financial resources. We should relook how we structure and execute our educational system so that we can tweak it here and there not for greater excellence in curriculum, but for greater equality in outcome.

Question: Is it worrying that our sense of national identity is very much tied to economic pragmatism, economic success and material success? Are we able to build an identity that is beyond pragmatism?

HKP: I don't believe that whatever national identity we have today is due to economic pragmatism. I think that the appreciation for Mr Lee Kuan Yew as an individual was very much tied in to the fact that he took this whole country from poverty to economic wealth. That gives us gratitude towards the PAP, or Lee Kuan Yew but it's not what binds us together.

What is interesting about identity is that it's often not a sense of who you are, but who you are not. You know you don't belong in places you don't belong in. And somehow, when you're home, you know you're home. Not because there's a big national identity ablaze out there, it's because this is where your friends are, this is where you grew up in. The markers of identity are very ambiguous, it's not worthwhile for us to try and define it, whether it's durian, chicken rice or any particular values. Those of us who've done NS, and those women in the future who I've advocated will do NS, their love for this country is not simply because we think our GDP is highest in the world. That's part of why we feel grateful. But it does not define us.

Question: Why do we think that Singaporeans consistently have the least engaged employees in Asia? What do you think is this future narrative towards work that we need to have so that we can bring the best of Singapore to contribute to our community?

HKP: The indexes show that we are supposedly a less engaged people than Thai people, and Indonesians. We don't know the quality of the surveys. But we should recognise that we are a hard driving people. If you look at the Indonesians and the Thais, there is a lot more to life than work. For us, work is probably the source of a lot of emotional satisfaction. And that's not necessarily bad; that's what took us from third world to first world. In terms of the future of work, we must not make the mistake of thinking that more engagement with your life would mean necessarily working less hard. I think working hard and our work ethic is important. What is important that I see today in the millennial generation, is that they're hardworking and will put in a lot of time of their own, but for things that they believe in. So the onus is partly on employers to try to engage young people so that they can give off their best.

Question: Did the content and tone of your speech today change following the passing of Lee Kuan Yew?

HKP: That's quite an insightful question. Of course I changed a part of my talk, as anyone would, when an important social event has occurred. If you're trying to be relevant, you have to make reference to that event. But my basic messages have stayed the same.

The messages are: what we need to do to increase cohesive diversity in our society, to increase social mobility, to ensure that the whole notion of identity is something you create of your own and there is no single Singapore identity. Mr Lee's passing, and the fact that he has in so many ways created our identity and created Singapore society, serves as a very poignant backdrop against which we now talk about identity.

Question: Do you think Singapore is ready for a non-Chinese Prime Minister? And if we are so ready, and we do get one, how will this appointment affect us as a country in the international standings, how would other countries view us, especially now that we have close ties with China and Taiwan?

HKP: Was America ready for a black President? The jury is out. But I think the fact that America had a black President — the first time they ever had one — says a lot for that society.

I actually believe we are ready, or will be ready soon. I do not think that the Singapore of tomorrow, the Singapore that I see among my children, and their friends, will differentiate on the basis of race or colour. They will be, clearly, making differentiations on the basis of views and so on.

However, I would also be realistic and say that if you had two persons of roughly equal calibre, and one was Chinese and one was Indian or Malay, who would win? I would say, you would probably have to recognise that there are going to be racial affinities. But if a leading party, like the PAP, were to put up a non-Chinese Prime Minister, would the country accept it? I think yes. Would the party lose its power, simply because they have a non-Chinese Prime Minister? I honestly believe, and I hope to be naïve enough to believe that if that person was of calibre, we would accept this. We already have a Deputy Prime Minister who is not Chinese who is extremely popular.

As to whether other countries would have problems with us if we had a non-Chinese Prime Minister, my answer is I would certainly hope that's not going to be the basis for consideration amongst us Singaporeans. We are a sovereign country, we should elect leaders whom we believe in. Our relationship with China is not determined by the racial affinity of our leadership.

Question: In the recent Cabinet reshuffle there were news headlines proclaiming that from one, there are now two Malay full ministers in Cabinet. Should the race of a capable man being promoted be relevant? When it comes to public housing, are we confident enough in the Singaporean identity that regardless of race, we can live together as Singaporeans, and we don't have to engineer our neighbourhoods so that it is a reflection of the different racial groups, but is just a reflection of us — Singaporeans?

HKP: My comment here is a nuanced one. I do not think it was necessarily bad for the government to indicate that we have now have got two Malays in Cabinet. I think we should blur the CMIO categorisations in our own minds and in how we define people so that we have a more richness of definition of ethnic diversity. But the danger here, which I would clearly not recommend, is that blurring CMIO categories, it becomes an excuse for a majority race to no longer be cognisant of the fact that minorities have to be very consciously supported in terms of their presence in the Cabinet and leadership positions elsewhere.

The flipside of blurring CMIO categorisation is to say: race doesn't matter anymore. It's a real danger that we must be very clear about. We must go beyond a simplistic CMIO model but that should never be the excuse to not be conscious of the need to send signals to the wider breadth of minorities in Singapore, that we are truly multiracial and multicultural and we walk the talk. Our actions must show the fact that diversity in Singapore is not just lip service but a living reality.

We must always preserve and protect the multiracialism that we have, but we must not just limit it to a category of four simplistic classifications.

Question: You mentioned the importance of strengthening cohesive diversity, especially with the emergence of new sub-ethnic groups. In future, we could have two extremes. The more optimistic scenario is where we embrace and become more welcoming of diversity and more towards the New York City type of model, and the not-so-good scenario could be where divisive diversity actually takes over. Which scenario do you think is more likely to happen in the next 50 years and can you elaborate on what's really at stake if the second scenario occurs?

HKP: I am an optimist. My sense of where Singapore is headed comes from my sense of younger people, who are today discussing the things that matter to them. I am totally confident that we are moving towards a more cohesive diversity. The civil society that I see rising out of Singapore today, gives me reason for encouragement. What could happen that would derail this and lead to divisive diversity is something that would not arise from the people themselves. I think if we get a government of the day — and I'm not referring to any party — which plays to the primal sentiments of an ethnic group to get votes and as a result inflames sentiments, this will result in a divisive diversity. But I do not fundamentally believe that it is in the inherent nature of people to be so discriminatory towards race, or differences. People tend to be generally inclusive, until their base instincts are aroused and manipulated. I am very optimistic that the cohesive diversity that I see coming out more and more in Singapore will be solidified in Singapore in the next 50 years.

HKP: Can I just say a few words?

I really truly just want to thank all of you. Here, the other room, and other people who have read the things I've done. It has been a very humbling exercise. You try it, and then you realise how much you didn't know about what you think you knew. It's been a humbling exercise, but more than anything else, I think we are truly on our way — all of us — whether you be in your 60s like me, or 30s or 20s, we're all on our way post Mr Lee Kuan Yew, who has truly given us such an incredible foundation and a base on which to build the next 50 years. And I feel incredibly privileged to have been able to share time with all of you, and to hope that this whole process of enriching our society, will continue for many, many more years to come. So thank you for this great privilege.

About the Cover Illustrator:

Audrey Yeo is a final year motion media design student at the Savannah College of Art and Design. She enjoys illustrating and riding her bicycle (not at the same time).

About the Chapters Illustrator:

Dorothy Hwee is a concept artist at Bandai Namco Studios who loves art, making video games and iced teh tarik. She also enjoys people watching at cafés but has occasionally been chased away for looking mildly creepy.

www.ingramcontent.com/pod-product-compliance
Lightning Source LLC
Chambersburg PA
CBHW071104280326
41928CB00051B/2821